Love Works deeply resonated with me on many levels. It's rare to find a guide that not only explores conscious leadership but does so with such vulnerability and heart. Your insights into leading with love, conscious capitalism, and the importance of the circular economy really struck a chord with me, as they align with my values and the way I approach my work. You've brilliantly woven together personal stories, thought-provoking concepts, and practical strategies that inspire readers to reflect and take action.

The balance of these elements makes your book both compelling and essential for anyone seeking to lead with purpose. I'm certain I'll be applying its lessons in my own nonprofit work. Your pioneering approach in the corporate world, particularly as a female, heart-centered leader, is something I believe will inspire many others to do the same.

This book is an invaluable resource for leaders who wish to create meaningful impact by embracing both compassion and innovation.

—Jenna McEwan,
Founder of Water4Life Global

After many years in the C-suite and Boardroom, this book really opened my eyes to some new concepts.

—Margaret Dano,
Board Director at Douglass Dynamics

In *Love Works*, Kelly invites us into a sacred dance, where Love becomes our guiding mantra. This creative act isn't just a gentle echo; it's a powerful shift that can awaken our consciousness and transform our work lives. By welcoming Love into the space of commerce, we can reimagine the fabric of capitalism, weaving in authentic awareness to address the profound challenges we face on this planet. Kelly's soft yet compelling invitation to embody Love as our essence has illuminated my path, allowing me to shift the power dynamics around me. It helps me align my intentions with contributions that resonate deeply within the business realm, revealing the infinite possibilities that life and capitalism have to offer.

—Zoey Powers,
Policy Advocate and Change Maker

Finally... a book that can change work for everyone! The stories in *Love Works* helped me reconsider culture and ways of working for my new business and team. Kelly shows the way with heartfelt experiences that made me laugh and cry, and her practical ideas offered along the way are now in my toolbox forever. I'm excited to join her in leaving this world better through conversation and connection. It's time for caring company cultures to rebuild caring communities.

—Rod Gibson,
Founder of Artesian Streams

Love Works is a truly transformative read that weaves together heart-felt narratives that inspire action, alongside insights that give readers the courage to lead with a human touch. Kelly's authentic voice shines through on every page, extending an invitation to infuse love into every facet of our lives, especially our work lives. Reading this book felt like an honest, heart-to-heart conversation with Kelly. Her vision of creating compassionate, connected workplaces is a much needed phenomenon in the world of work today. Anyone looking to elevate their leadership game through genuine care and fierce inclusion should grab a copy of this book. Having worked with Kelly, I can say for certain that the pages of this book are intentionally curated based out of a truly lived experience.

—Rhea OngYiu,
Director at Ernst Young, Transforming Enterprises
with Human-Centered Approach

Kelly Winegarden Hall's story is one of inspiration. This book shares her vision for how taking LOVE into the workplace and into our daily lives can fill us with JOY. Chapter 4: Activating Love was one of my favorite chapters. It reconfirmed a lot of what I try to do each day I step foot into my school building. It left me feeling more energized and motivated to continue expressing love for those I work with by simply by being kind, caring, compassionate, and by showing a level of concern that some people never see in their work environments.

—Anthony Dean,
SPED Teacher & President of the Washington Township Education Association

Love Works boldly embraces the act of bringing our love to work instead of sequestering it at home. Kelly Hall cracks open the traditional definition of love and offers specific, actionable steps to create, with love, a compassionate, safe and connected workplace. If you are looking for an innovative and inspiring way to foster abundance and fulfillment for everyone this book is an invaluable resource.

—Shawna Reininger,
The Conscious Enterprise

Kelly Hall poignantly describes and encourages a work environment that embodies the directive "treat others as you would like to be treated." Caring for the "whole individual" at work, as opposed to the "employee" will add super power behind the mission of any organization. Requiring this book to be read in business schools will result in better teams, better missions, and a better world.

—Joanna Genser,
Former CFO and Chairmen of the Board, Intown Cares

In *Love Works*, Kelly Hall draws on her remarkable career and life experiences to reveal a transformative approach to the workplace: integrating genuine care and personal connection. With warmth and insight, Hall demonstrates how infusing compassion and authentic curiosity about others into professional settings can foster creative, high-performing, harmonious teams. By prioritizing meaningful relationships, team members not only elevate their work but also cultivate a vibrant, fulfilling atmosphere where everyone can thrive.

This inspiring guide shows how bringing love into the workplace can unleash creativity, strengthen bonds, and create a truly rewarding career for all. *Love Works* is a must-read for anyone looking to reshape the modern workplace into a space of purpose, fulfillment, and inclusive collaboration.

—Sean Kennedy,
Social Entrepreneur

One of the things I most admire about Kelly is how, while leading a $1.5 billion division of a Fortune 50 company, she took the principles I shared with her about the power of trust and exponentially improved outcomes at all levels (for herself, her direct team, her division, and the companies she has worked for) by integrating those ideas with what she discovered about the power of love. Kelly's insights here about psychological safety, extending trust, and deliberate empowerment align perfectly with what I've written about effective change leadership. What Kelly shares about living and working L.A.R.G.E. takes everything I've learned about culture, strategy execution, and personal and organizational effectiveness to the next level. *Love Works* has reshaped the way I think about the time I've been given to make a difference in today's VUCA world.

—Andy Cindrich,
Author, Coach and Keynote Speaker

Having worked with Kelly—I can say that love did work! She always managed to maximize engagement and inclusivity in our teams. She has captured the essence of this in *Love Works*. I sincerely hope more leaders give her approach a try!

—Mark Kleinschmit,
COO Other Half Processing

I've had the pleasure of holding space for Kelly during a part of her remarkable healing journey.

Her message is particularly important and timely, especially in an era when darkness often seems to overshadow the light. It is a message of love and hope that can only be authentically conveyed by someone who has navigated through darkness and emerged stronger on the other side.

Rooted in the practicality of love, her message is both effective and sustainable. Kelly's work and life have challenged and inspired me to look beyond the limitations of my own narrative, encouraging me to become a more loving and expansive leader.

—Dimitri Mugianis,
Cardea Founder, Ceremonialist & Harm Reduction Community Organizer

As a private equity investor, I am keenly aware of the impact culture has on any company's results. *Love Works* is full of interesting stories and actionable insights that made me pause to reflect on my own behaviors as a leader of leaders.

Hall is a gifted storyteller, weaving thoughtful principles into each chapter that will resonate and inspire readers to bring meaningful change into their everyday lives. A master at relating these 'common sense' ideas, Hall provides a relatable and applicable guide to reframe safety, redistribute power and activate bigger, bolder wins.

—Jack Glover,
Managing Partner - Incline Equity

LOVE WORKS

TRANSFORMING THE WORKPLACE WITH PURPOSE AND AUTHENTICITY

KELLY WINEGARDEN HALL

Love Works

Cover Design by Christian Rafetto (www.humblebooksmedia.com)

Published in association with The Fedd Agency, Inc., a literary agency.

Fedd Books
P.O. Box 341973
Austin, TX 78734
www.thefeddagency.com

Paperback ISBN: 9781964508283

Library of Congress Control Number: 2024922324

First Edition

Printed in the United States.

DEDICATION

For every boss, colleague, supplier, customer, and coach I met through work and now call a friend.

For tomorrow's capitalists, may your loving leadership shape a new normal.

For Jack, Kate, Anne, and Tyler, who've filled my life with the best of bottomless, abundant, and unconditional love.

For Grandpa Leland, Grandma & Grandpa Conner, Mom, and Dad who showed me how to leverage education, effort, service, and celebration to enjoy this amazing life.

TABLE OF CONTENTS

FOREWORD: LOVE WORKS by Helen Mets

The concept of "love" at work may, at first, seem counterintuitive. For so long, the business world has taught us to focus on goals, profits, and productivity as the ultimate measures of success. But what Kelly Hall beautifully illustrates is that when love becomes a part of our guiding principles, it accelerates performance and it deepens impact. It is through love that we cultivate trust, inspire loyalty, and build teams that thrive, not just in numbers but in spirit. It is through love that we see people not merely as colleagues or clients, but as individuals with dreams, fears, and the potential to create something remarkable.

I have had the privilege to work with Kelly for over fifteen years and to personally witness her incredible impact. The philosophy that she outlines in her book is not just a theory for Kelly; it is a way of life that she embodies every day. As a cancer survivor, her journey is a testament to the power of resilience, empathy, and unwavering commitment to making a positive impact. She shares stories from her own career, illustrating how love and compassion have been instrumental in her success and the success of those around her. Her insights and experiences offer valuable lessons for anyone looking to find fulfillment and success in both their professional and personal lives.

What I found in these pages were stories of leaders who dared to bring compassion into their boardrooms, visionaries who believed that empathy and respect should guide every decision, and teams who built their success not only on talent but on kindness and mutual respect. These are not just idealistic tales but real accounts of how love has transformed businesses, communities, and lives.

Perhaps the most moving aspect of *Love Works* is that it challenges each of us to see love not only as a feeling but as a choice—a series of actions we take every day. Whether it's the way we listen to a colleague, the patience we show during difficult conversations, or the encouragement we offer when someone needs it most, love can be an active, deliberate part of our lives. This book reminds us that love is not merely an emotion; it is a commitment to act with integrity, empathy, and purpose, regardless of the circumstances.

As you begin this journey through *Love Works*, I invite you to let go of any preconceptions about love as "soft" or impractical. Allow yourself to consider that love is, in fact, a powerful force capable of driving success and creating fulfillment beyond what metrics and titles could ever measure. Let these stories inspire you, and may they remind you that the true value of any work lies not only in what we achieve but in how we choose to get there.

Love Works is more than just a book. It is a call to action, a gentle but insistent reminder that our lives and our work can be elevated in remarkable ways when we lead with love. I hope you, too, are as moved by these pages as I was, and that you find, as I did, a new way to bring love into everything you do.

PROLOGUE

"What can I do to leave the world better than I found it before I go?"

I've pondered this question daily since May 2022—seven months after a metastatic breast cancer diagnosis and one year before a five-year expatriate contract to serve as managing director of Niaga would end. The stage was set for change: I was forty-eight years old, a twice-divorced empty nester with two kids in college, sensing the sunset of my life. With twenty-five years of business experience chasing impact in thirty-five countries, I'd experienced highs and lows of leadership, business teams, economic cycles, and myself.

Living in Europe had provided beautiful contrasts to my daily life in the United States. For example, Dutch colleagues commonly start their careers with twenty-five days of paid vacation, and they enjoy multiple two-to-three week breaks per year. In fact, it was a policy violation to ask any employee to take less than two weeks of holidays at a time! Even with these extended rest and recovery breaks, Dutch teams accomplished the same amount of output in a full year as a typical American team that worked more hours, brought computers on short vacations to respond to emails, and participated in an important call (or ten) while trying to prioritize friends and family.

I will share several stories from Niaga in the chapters ahead. Niaga is the word 'again' spelled backward, reflecting a mission to 'design with the end in mind,' to build everyday things like carpets, mattresses, and furniture in a way that all materials can be recovered and reused again and again at the end of a product's useful life. These three household goods represent the top ten contributors to bulky landfill waste. Our team and our partners were creating processes, materials, patent protection, and proof for recovery and recycling methods.

The joys I experienced working with diverse colleagues in our high-empowerment, high-risk innovation venture were only dampered by the fractured and failing systems I observed in the news, on the streets, and around the world. There is so much **dis-ease**[1] everywhere, with COVID-19 and climate change demanding global attention in surround sound. What could I do in weeks, months, and years, not decades, to contribute to better lives for as many people as possible?

A diagnosis limiting the chapters left in my story was, in the end, a remarkable gift. Feeling a positive pressure to live my best life now, I prioritized things I love with people I love, including my work. I chose gratitude daily, noticing I'm still here while others are dying somewhere each minute of every day. I returned to the United States and moved closer to my family. I simplified my life and meditated each day in search of direction. How could I use my remaining **lifetime** to affect

[1] Throughout this book, 'dis-ease' is used intentionally instead of 'disease.' While disease is defined as 'a disorder with a commonly understood set of symptoms,' dis-ease is offered to mean 'the state of not being at ease.'

positive change to the maximum extent possible? Why have I had the unique experiences that have shaped my life? In the end, will my life have mattered?

With a little space from the daily grind, it became easy to see where my experiences could be useful to others. I've been a colleague who works ***with*** people, not over them. I've successfully attacked the sources of disease in my body, my life, and my teams. Beyond a shadow of a doubt, I now know that capitalism, trust, and love are three incredibly powerful forces in our world. It may sound strange to put capitalism next to the values of trust and love, but by the time you finish this book, you'll recognize how powerful care, compassion, and connection can be in offices, factories, and boardrooms. If only we could pause to discuss how much better things could be—so quickly—if all people brought their love to work with intention, abundance, and authenticity.

In the documentary *The Pursuit*, Arthur Brooks makes the case for capitalism as a force to lift billions of people out of poverty. At a time when the 'C' word triggers flashbacks to layoffs, plant closures, lost benefits, 24/7 schedules, income inequality, outsourcing, offshoring, inflation, lost pensions, natural resource exploitation, manipulative marketing, and more, I still believe the single best opportunity to create balance and positive change is to do our work differently.

Adults around the world spend the greatest portion of their lives working. We exchange our time and talents for money to pay our bills, educate ourselves and our children, create experiences that turn into our memories, and fill our homes with the artifacts of our lives. How much better could life be if we always looked forward to the next shift, inspired to create and deliver solutions, products, and outcomes with leaders and teammates we trusted to have our best interests at heart?

How different would it be if great debates, which pushed each other's buttons and crossed lines occasionally, were always followed by a trust talk, exploration, and apology if needed?

I am a Loving Leader and Loving Teammate—proud to know the colleagues, customers, and partners I've shared space and time with over the years. I'm here to share stories from our ventures and adventures, as helping just five companies shift from hierarchical power dynamics to maximum engagement and empowerment everywhere would make this effort worthwhile. There's a remarkable surge in productivity and results when energy is activated at every level of an organization. Deeply inclusive and powerfully collaborative organizations bring more to work, home, and communities. I can promise only good things are in store for companies that align every teammate's intellectual horsepower with their motivation through loving connection.

The values I've always brought to work are the same ones that restored my health. By systematically addressing every source of disease in life, we can be healthier, happier, and more interconnected as humans. I call it living and working L.A.R.G.E.—embracing Love, Abundance, Respect, Gratitude, and Equality as a way of being. This book is not about nutrition, movement, mindset, or recovery—all essential to optimal human function and things I also have passion for. This book is about the most powerful force in the universe and the potential to use it where we spend most of our time to create better companies, better communities, better countries, better lives, and a better world FOR ALL.

The world is devastatingly out of balance in modern times. We are consuming the world's natural resources at an alarming pace. Waste and pollution are accumulating and affecting our climate and our health. Food and water supplies are in flux and falling in quantity and quality, affecting humans, animals, plants, and all living things. Fear, anxiety, worry, shame, and blame separate us from each other and from our gifts and our grace. **Until they don't**.

It is time to try something new.

I am ready to pause with as many of the world's leaders and workers as I can to talk about love as the driving force behind conscious capitalism. Together, we can forge a path to eliminate so much pain and waste in our world.

A publisher encouraged me to be crystal clear about the audience I care to activate most with this book. I have chosen to seek the attention of business leaders and people leaders, as I believe we hold the greatest capacity at this moment in time to activate lasting change.

In 2024, it's easy to see progress as stakeholders demand change on environmental, social, and governance issues. But even with climate action, environmental cleanups, waste reduction, and energy transitions, so many companies relentlessly prioritize shareholder returns first. This imbalance creates great wealth for a few, good lives for many, and disrupted lives for those who lose their roles or have their lives otherwise affected by restructuring actions. We are taking from the planet's resources without replenishing the stores. Employees give their time and energy to create and deliver with constant pressure to do more with less, grow at any cost, negotiate until it hurts, deliver faster, and connect 24/7. An undercurrent of fear and anxiety pervades psyches and households over healthcare costs, financial insecurity, and tightly restricted time. Constant coping and chasing leads to overwhelmed bodies and minds buzzing from dopamine, cortisol, and adrenaline.

Vibrant and inclusive systems can deliver excellent shareholder returns without negatively affecting employees, customers, suppliers, and communities. In the long run, higher participation in the workforce and more people with resources to meet basic needs—let alone enjoy their lifetimes—can reduce crime, celebrate diversity, expand abundance, reduce dependence, and extend care to vulnerable neighbors.

How do we boldly course-correct and powerfully pivot to deeply conscious company cultures? How do we enable caring and connected organizations to drive profoundly positive effects, one pay period after another—until fierce inclusion, radical transparency, and deep satisfaction are simply normal?

Redistributing power and soothing separation starts with curiosity and dialogue ABOUT our differences to open our minds and free our spirits. The smallest shifts in attention and connection at work can activate creativity, stimulate innovation, and empower participation in problem-solving. With the courage to talk with individuals or entire supply chains about unmet needs, frustrations, issues, and opportunities, we can address toxic and wasteful systems. We can shift to circular and abundant markets, attract breakthroughs, and quickly adopt effective, efficient, and sustainable solutions.

In the long run, we might not need so many armies and prisons to protect and defend loving people from each other. This is certainly an ambitious dream for an increasingly volatile and polarized humanity, and I'll make the case that love is the key to opening the floodgates of positive change.

While I believe solutions exist for all challenges, this book focuses on change that serves working adults around the world. These pages hold short stories and actionable ideas to help any individual or organization pivot today to improve engagement, expand empowerment, enhance performance, and deliver better results.

As quickly as possible, we need all hands on deck to innovate. Creative solutions to challenges in each corner of the world should come from those closest to the problems. When our team at Niaga wanted to ensure all components in any product we created could be reused, we empowered our chemists to identify materials with properties fit for mechanical and chemical recycling. When we realized digital passports would be needed to document the ingredients in things, as labels provide transparency for ingredients in our food, we collaborated with track and trace experts from other companies and software designers. We have the tools to lead change, like gemba walks, kaizen improvements, design workshops, continuous improvement efforts, and problem-solving programs. We can empower teams and activate communities, place our hands on each other's backs while we all see, sort, and solve.

It's time to pause to dramatically enhance the quality of our dialogue and ask more than we tell. It's time to celebrate positive deviants, those among us who have already achieved top employee engagement, served extremely satisfied customers, delivered perfect safety records, and driven years of strong performance without restructurings and layoffs. Let's celebrate the firms and organizations where everyone participates, voices are heard, creativity is encouraged, and quality of life is treasured. Let's share these stories and copy and paste, rinse and repeat.

I have witnessed and enjoyed fiercely inclusive and radically transparent business teams. Where customers were partners and employees were teammates. Where scores were settled with courageous conversations and shared responsibility for win-win outcomes. Where diversity was an asset and psychological safety was assured. Where fights were allowed, and trust was restored. It can happen. It has happened. We can all enjoy that energy, that passion, and those results just as much as we loved working so hard for the changes we chased and dreams we longed to deliver.

I offer these stories, which can be read in any order, as food for thought and stimulus for change. Please explore with me and consider bringing more of your love to work. Ask what the loving version of us should do in any situation. Visit the loveworks.world website along the way to share your experiences and ideas so we can leverage each other's experiences.

I am convinced the world will be better as we do!

1

WHY LOVE?

"I See You, and I Love You."

—HOFFMAN INSTITUTE COACH

Is there a more loaded word in any language than 'love'? This simple, four-letter word has profound power. It is sweet to one person and romantic to another. Private and conditional for Casey, light and open to Joe. Each of us relates to love in a different way, as our relationships with love are deeply personal, crafted from experiences starting at birth. We give our love, send our love, express our love, and withdraw our love.

What is love, really? We use the word to describe feelings, acts, and connections. Is love an energy, a bond, or a quality? Over the course of a single day, love can be a belief, a person, and a tennis score.

I've had a volatile journey with love. As a child of divorced parents, I believed love ends. Raised in Catholic traditions, love was a tangled mess of sinners and saints destined for Heaven, Purgatory or Hell. As a kid in rural Iowa, love followed hard work and completed chores. As a student and athlete, I associated performance and achievement with love.

My extended family isn't affectionate, so love came in the form of gifts and quality time more than touch or words. I absolutely enjoyed family, friends, teammates, and strangers while also never feeling as strong, pretty, worthy, or deserving as my peers.

Accepting love as conditional, I doubled down on being loveable and on the good side of the force—working overtime, saying yes to everything, entertaining generously, and smiling no matter what.

Twentyish years into adult life, the 'efforting' caught up to me. My family and my career had been the best and most rewarding parts of my life, and I was thriving as measured by happy kids, physical fitness, a busy social life, a beautiful home in a Cleveland suburb, and meaningful work as a corporate executive. Instantly, though, I tumbled into a deep emotional hole when one of my bosses asked me to resign from my job, deciding they would prefer someone else in my position. I'll be the first to admit this wasn't the best boss-subordinate relationship I've ever experienced, but I was blindsided by the action. Even though I was not being fired for cause, I was asked to leave the company that day, return my computer and files, and abandon a team I enjoyed. There was certainly only one acceptable answer to the firm request.

I had been on the other side of restructurings and layoffs, but this was my first and only experience receiving the awful news on a slow-motion day I'll never forget.

I felt a gaping hole in my heart, terrible embarrassment, and tremendous guilt. Overnight, I flipped from an accomplished, successful female leader and working mom to an unemployed person and lost soul who had missed so many games, meals, and moments with those I loved most. My second marriage was its own adventure, full of high highs and low lows, a tightrope one day and the sweetest treat the next. For weeks, I felt empty, anxious, and blue. All the money in the world couldn't have filled the hole in my heart or eased my pain, so anyone who believes severance checks make people feel better after being laid off or fired is simply wrong.

At this juncture, I hated how I felt and sought help. I found myself at a week-long retreat offered by the Hoffman Institute, isolated from phones, televisions, and radios. Billy Bush had gone through the Hoffman Institute's program after losing his job when the Trump "Grab her by the [you-know-what]" scandal cost him his job as a television host, and he was featured in an article about the Hoffman Process. Through his experience with the program, Billy found his own role, responsibility, and peace in the crazy series of events that led to his termination while Donald Trump ascended to the United States presidency. If Billy Bush could feel grateful and whole after that kind of crazy, maybe I could, too.

It was time to reset, and I unplugged from all outside influences for a full week to strictly follow the Hoffman program at a nature resort in Connecticut. In the first hour of the first day, a coach found me and offered me a piece of fruit. They said, "I see you, and I love you." At this moment, I simply choked back my laughter, thinking, "*WHAT? That's utterly ridiculous. You don't even know me, and if you did, you wouldn't love me for long.*"

This week changed my life forever. At the end of the program, the same person gave me a piece of fruit and said, "I see you, and I love you" again. To which I could genuinely reply, "Thank you! I see you as well, and I love you, too." This was the week I learned love is not currency. It is not traded, bartered, given, or taken. It is our very life force. It is abundant, flowing, and accessible to anyone, anywhere, at any time. All I had to do to enjoy love was to believe it, give it, and receive it. I cannot tell you more about the program without violating their very special, thoughtful cadence of activity and reflection, but you can learn more about it at thehoffmaninstitute.com.

Today, I'm offering to reframe love as a state of consciousness and awareness more than a temporary act or gesture. Love as an abundant, flowing and universally good force to be shared and enjoyed by anyone and everyone. Love is activated in relationships and is the most comfortable and natural force that has ever been and ever will be. In fact, any sensations that are not easy, warm, or effortless in relationships are simply contrasts to love. These feelings are information, letting us know shifts are needed to restore ease and return to love. This love belongs everywhere and is equally powerful in the boardroom as in the bedroom.

I've been asked not to use the word 'love' at work on multiple occasions. This is quite possibly the worst advice I've ever heard. Who benefits from restricting or withholding passion, compassion, commitment, and connection in commercial ecosystems? Perhaps people who want to feel better about their "tough decisions" that negatively affect others.

The force behind my thriving relationships with colleagues and customers has always been love. The genuine joy I find in collaborating, driving positive change, offering solutions to problems, and overcoming challenges with others is fueled by my care and appreciation for them. I bathe in the compassion, connection, and satisfaction that flow back to me from them.

Yes, products and services are sold and delivered, and money flows between our firms. But the effort and work on the hardest days are not painful as much as purposeful and productive. We are selling our time and energy to our companies in exchange for pay, and we create, innovate, produce, solve, and deliver in return.

Rediscovering and reframing love has shifted my relationship with power. Before this pivotal time, I held beliefs reinforced by hierarchical systems. I believed the chiefs, generals, presidents, and vice presidents were the big people holding power and worth the most in the organization. This status was consistent with their decision rights, positions on podiums, nice cars, business class seats, and large homes in gated communities. I looked up to them and wanted to be breathing their air and similarly situated someday. I enjoyed my own space in the middle, proud to support, coach, and develop the humans in my care. But yes, if I am completely honest, I felt larger than my subordinates and superior to them as their supervisor on paper. All these systems were reinforced in my communities and social circles, as people introduced themselves with their title and led with their jobs before any other attribute of their identity.

When my entire existence was turned upside down, I filled out my first forms at schools, doctors' offices, and registrations without an occupation. Unable to check "full-time" or "part-time" for employment status, I had to figure out who I really was in this life, in humanity. I couldn't be more grateful for this karmic kick in the ass or for the profound changes in the past eight years of my life.

Through the journey out of that dark shadow, I found the truth: All humans are fundamentally equal. We are simply souls and spirits in human bodies, given one lifetime that unfolds for everyone one day at a time. We each enjoy one life force powering us in the generous present moment, and every single body will expire at the end of each human experience. Like every living thing in the world, we require air, water, food, rest, and relationships to thrive.

As with every living thing in the world, humans flourish when conditions are most supportive of flow with the best environments: living aligned with nature and our nature, giving and receiving care, and connecting in kindness and compassion. When systems are organized around these fundamentals, we all have access to even higher states of existence: awe, wonder, joy, magic, and miracles.

I make a conscious choice every day to live my best life in love. I bring that love to myself and my miraculous, self-healing body. I bring that love to my relationships. I also bring that love to work, as it's a joy and a pleasure to create great things with colleagues, customers, and suppliers. When I encounter others who are competitive, playing a win-lose game, highly critical/ judgmental, or wrapped up in their own power paradigms, I may feel a strong impulse and friction in my body or mind. But I respond with compassion for their humanity while I reach for grace and understanding. These humans are not mine to fix but to appreciate silently while I love myself enough to cope, care, and choose to live in love, at ease.

My dream is to stimulate a series of pauses for reflection and dialogue. I'd like to stop for a moment and reconsider the stories we are activating, reinforcing, and spreading that separate, restrict, and hurt people. While most people act in their best interest and do their best every day, it's easy to see rampant **dis-ease** in our lives, organizations, countries, and planet. We accept fear and anxiety as normal states to cope with while we eat empty calories and wash them down with cocktails that numb the pain and calm the nerves. When our bodies and minds have had enough, we take drugs and undergo procedures to treat the symptoms chemically and mechanically. All this expensive and exhausting "care" when we haven't addressed the underlying conditions or paused to question how we live our lives and treat each other.

At fifty-one years old, I've made plenty of mistakes and hurt people I've loved as many times as I've been hurt myself. I've faced cancer three times. I've identified as an American and weathered the U.S. political chaos. I've identified as Spiritual-Not Religious and a forever Hawkeye.

Others have called me Mom, Ex, Boss Lady, Baby, and Bitch. It has taken five decades to realize that these are all stories, illusions, and lenses that only serve to separate me from my true self and from others. Releasing my attachment to my labels and programming and embracing a new role as a skeptical student of my stories has allowed me a new life, waking each day as 100% human and 100% divine—just as I see everyone else. Ease has flowed into my body and my life as I address **dis-ease** at every juncture.

I have finally reached a state where my spirit is stronger than my stories. I want everything good for myself, for you, and for every other human. As I live L.A.R.G.E., being Love, Abundance, Respect, Gratitude, and Equality, I want you to have it, too. As I enjoy freedom, I want everyone else to have it, too. As I enjoy loving connections to strangers, nature, music, and food, I want this joy for everyone.

Did we meet on the hamster wheel? Surely, you have also ridden the roller coaster of downturns, outsourcing, plant closures, mergers, and exits. Hopefully, you've also joyously collaborated, created, delivered, and cashed big checks. Maybe we've watched and admired leaders and owners who do care, prioritize safety, and empower and enable others. Perhaps you've also observed a leading class of investors whose abundance came from fixing distressed businesses, investing in communities, and celebrating the teams who delivered on purpose, profit, and people.

It's time to ask everyone to stand up and take a fresh look around collectively. Today, let's use our **lifetimes and our companies to reset agendas and change the way we work**. Total shareholder return is just not enough. Environmental, social, and governance activities and reports are not enough. It's time to bring our love to work with 5-factor wins (see Chapter 14) in mind. Our agendas can prioritize thriving employees who love serving our customers. Customers who pay the bills fund everything inside of a good enterprise. Paid bills are an expression of gratitude for goods and services received, and loyalty comes as happy people exchange their abundance to receive something they want and need from the firm. We use that money to express our gratitude to the employees contributing time, energy, and passion to enable research and development, production, and delivery of goods and services. When happy and fulfilled employees return to their homes and communities, they buy goods and services in their lives and enjoy their leisure time with loved ones. Vibrant communities exist where people have the resources to participate in education, arts, and entertainment served by people who offer their gifts to the world. When we are actively curating culture, nurturing passion, and activating empowerment, love flows into and around every nook and cranny of our lives.

Let's work together to attack separation. With urgency, let's deliver for all humans, the planet, and future generations. Let's eliminate dis-ease, pain, abusive power, and pollution. Maybe it's time to question why we need so many policies and procedures to protect ourselves from each other and why we use any life force to hurt anyone else, let alone kill them.

Love is the most powerful force in the universe, and the only things in the way of bringing love to work are our resistance to true equality, our addiction to status, and our perception of scarcity. Nature and the planet provide the resources to feed and house eight billion people every day. Earth has the same miraculous self-healing capability as our own bodies when we respect and care for her. Every soul enjoying a human experience has time, energy, emotions, and ideas. The parks, museums, aquariums, zoos, artists, chefs, athletes, actors, and entertainers of the world offer spaces and places to experience the awe and wonders of life. Our human senses are meant to be open to beauty, pleasure, texture, flavor, and sound to love all of life and each other along the way. It's an utter tragedy we are taking more than we give. We are polluting our bodies, our waterways, and our fields. We are patching crevasses with Band-Aids when activating connection and welcoming everyone to the party could rebalance and restore resources, soothe the wounds of separation, and unleash the right to life for all.

I propose activating conscious capitalism today. The fastest transformations start with redistributing power, resetting priorities, and welcoming love into culture. Loving Leaders pursue, manage, and measure performance against 100% safe operations, 100% employee engagement, 100% customer satisfaction, 100% quality, 100% on-time and complete, 0% harm, 0% waste, and 100% resource replenishment. Loving employees show up on time to tackle projects, build products, deliver services, and invest in each other. We see each other, protect each other, and hold space for honest dialogue and extensive positive change.

A book on conscious consumption can follow another day, as a balanced and sustainable world may be enabled by conscious capitalism, but it's only realized when we individually participate, trade our time and energy, and just take what we need. If we want less **dis-ease,** we must nourish our bodies with natural foods, get proper rest, connect in loving kindness, and play and laugh a lot more.

These pages offer stories of my professional life and learnings I've extracted as examples of activated change. At the end of most chapters, you'll find suggestions to activate Loving Leadership and Loving Employment in your life. Use these ideas and tools as you wish, and please share your own stories of impact as we enable a world every human can enjoy. There is no greater place than work to empower change and activate abundance for all. Let's do it in love, and always #bettertogether.

2

SAFETY FIRST

Workplace safety = physical and psychological safety

Would you believe me if I told you every single day is Bring Your Family to Work Day?

I believe this one insight could address half the diversity, inclusion, and equity issues lingering in our modern human experience. By understanding the power of human stories, we curate space for everyone to be perfectly equal in exercising programmed preferences, also known as our personal normal.

While some leaders push, pull, and police to drive consistency and control, Loving Leaders leverage tolerance and curiosity to unleash the full potential of every teammate in their care. We realize everyone is the center of their own universe and seeks autonomy, happiness, fairness, and freedom. We understand that most people like their ideas most, and humans like to say yes when asked for help. We let it get messy and teach people to apologize, repair, restore, and explore. We realize psychological safety is just as important as physical safety in getting the most out of the people we work with each day.

At several points, the self-organized teams at Niaga found themselves at odds, pinched between differences of opinion and dividing into corners for a battle royale. We had a diverse, experienced, purpose-driven crew. Some strong personalities were biased to force and aggressiveness, others had deeply calm and quiet observation skills, and others brought uncanny scientific curiosity requiring space to test and to prove ideas and concepts. Some colleagues deeply trusted their intuition, treasuring speed over precision, and others wanted to measure twice or thrice to act once. This diversity led to some serious disagreements from time to time. As the head coach, I was called upon to sort the shit and soothe the souls.

On one occasion, a relatively forceful leader unilaterally decided to place a crucial pilot asset under lockout-tagout hold while we evaluated internal compliance requirements for our new corporate owner. This FULL STOP threatened business development, with two partners on a great path to launch products in the months ahead. These crucial, hard-won first orders were mission-critical to a startup venture that hadn't turned a profit yet.

Whether this decision was right or wrong, the WAY the decision had been made sent two collaborating teams into a spiral. The intensity escalated to frustration and anger so high that a few colleagues vocally considered quitting. After observing the pain, I organized an intervention: a deliberate pause to talk about what had happened, why it unfolded the way it did, and how it made people feel. Each teammate was asked to reflect on their own experience and to respond to each other's feelings.

Over the course of two hours, the team climate, which had become fiery hot for some and ice cold to others, returned to a more comfortable zone for all. We discussed what we learned from the breakdown, how we would avoid it next time, and committed to a path forward. Within six weeks, the team was back to delivering milestones together. More important, though, was that the skills to experience chaos and restore trust came forth again and again later. Hands that may have been waving or clenched in fists returned to the others' backs where they belonged.

Why do we react and respond in ways that shock, surprise, and hurt each other sometimes?

When faced with conflict or pain, our automatic behaviors are very instinctual. Patterns and programs were stored subconsciously throughout our childhoods as we observed adults around us, experienced punishments and rewards, and learned to navigate good, bad, right, and wrong responses at home and school. Everyone comes by their biases innocently, even if these 'right ways to be' make it difficult to play nicely with every person on every playground we encounter.

Generally, we can count on people to act in their best interest and with good intentions, but that doesn't mean harmony is guaranteed in any way, shape, or form. Too often, we enter conflict in confusion, longing to be heard, to be understood, and to be right in the end. Many discussions and debates are productive and fun when we have the energy and time to share ideas and evaluate the pros and cons of giving and taking together. However, things get messy when power paradigms reinforce the idea that some people are big, and some are small at the table. Quality of dialogue falls when we stop feeling valued and safe. Things break down quickly when we feel steamrolled or disregarded when things happen ***to*** us instead of ***with*** us.

I've watched myself and others "self-sort" into safe spaces again and again. We observe the patterns and paradigms around us and tuck into lanes that keep us out of harm's way. We give our time, energy, and focus to tasks while doing whatever it takes to feel good enough without being too much or too little. Our childhood homes and schools provided frameworks for performance and reward. It's easy enough to embrace our step on the ladder, whether we hold an entry-level hourly wage production job or responsibility for a team. We value ourselves with titles, wages, and status. Rarely do we see the common denominator: Every single human is one person with twenty-four hours in a day. No one gets more time, and no person's minute is longer or shorter than sixty seconds at a time. Do you value your own lifetime as much as you value your neighbor's or a celebrity's lifetime?

You see, every single human has five things in common: 1) A physical body—our personal vessel for experiencing the human form, created by two other humans; 2) A mind—the homo sapiens' unique capacity to think, organize, create, and communicate among the other creatures, shaped by our stories; 3) A spirit—the mysterious force observable in all living things; 4) **Lifetime**—the generous present moment to be consumed as we so desire; and 5) Death—There is a day our body expires, our human time expires, and our life force transitions to its next form.

With all this very solid, common ground, it's fascinating to observe the 10,000 ways we insist we are different: more, less, privileged, special, worthy, unworthy, smart, stupid, better, worse, bigger, smaller, important, unimportant, winners, losers, strong, weak, too much, not enough, falling short, or shining bright. What is a human if not a walking library of separating stories, gathered from birth and reinforced day-by-day as families domesticate us to "Our Tribe's Ways"? Eventually, the home stories are reinforced by the church stories. And then the school stories. Enter television stories, news stories, and social media stories. By the time anyone enters the workforce, they've gathered enough "I am..." descriptors for an entertaining autobiography.

If every great company, leader, and worker puts safety first, why are so many people fatigued, distracted, and anxious in their work lives? Adults in developed countries spend more time working than any other single activity between 25 and 65 years of age, and in these modern times, ~5,500 Americans and 3,300 Europeans die in workplace accidents. The U.S. Occupational Health and Safety Administration reports 2.7 injuries and illnesses per 100 workers in America. There is great progress in physical safety and some progress in workplace health and wellness. Well-being and mental health are rising on agendas as stress, loneliness, and depression penetrate people in every walk of life, bringing these states of dis-ease and discontent to home and to work.

I have the pleasure of working with Atlas Holdings, based in Greenwich, Connecticut, as a board member at one of their twenty-seven portfolio companies. With remarkable consistency, every—and I mean EVERY—meeting starts with a safety briefing, and each board meeting starts with safety performance. We do not just gloss over safety exits and fire drills planned for the day, recordable injury rates, and lost time accidents; at any meeting, we know where the defibrillators are, who is trained in CPR, who will call 911, which accidents have happened, what we learned, and how we're going to eliminate the possibility of it happening twice. Safety performance is recognized and celebrated, and environmental, health, and safety leaders have a seat at the table along with a responsibility to share best practices and learn.

Atlas holds an annual meeting in January of each year, bringing hundreds of Atlas leaders, management teams, board members, and operating partners, high-potential talent, and investors together to work and play. Progress, performance, and best practices are presented. We share, learn, and celebrate together, and topics relevant to advancing the portfolio agenda are advanced by leading experts in their fields.

Atlas has invested in presentations on generational dynamics and mental health in recent conferences, recognizing frightening trends in depression, drug use, and suicide. They are demonstrating care and compassion for the people in our companies and communities and equipping Loving Leaders to understand, connect, and support people in our whole lives.

I asked for time to address the audience in 2023. We had all heard the daily safety address and absorbed best practices in workplace safety from some of the portfolio's highest-risk operations. One element of workplace safety hit close to home for me, only enhanced by the mental health presentation in the agenda.

Doing any job well requires focus, and modern lives present forces that distract even the best of yogis from the task at hand. In my case, my cancer diagnosis was in mind. I showed up to work every day, between tests and scans and while waiting in anticipation of more information. I woke wondering if I was going to die, with my mind wandering to scenarios, my kids, and long-term dreams evaporating. I was present for every call, video conference, and meeting, but honestly, I wasn't present.

How many people in your company face a health crisis or love someone who is facing dis-ease or requiring special care? Who is going through a divorce or has a child with depression or a drug problem? Who faces financial challenges? Who lost a pet or is overwhelmed by life in general?

Loving teams practice K.F.C., a term I learned from my friend Tamara while we worked together many years ago. Know Me, Focus Me, Care about Me. Only when we have an open and safe space to share our whole selves will we know that Sarah should not have been on the forklift or crane the week her father had a stroke. Caring about a colleague's well-being means asking how things are going outside of work so no one faces their darkest days alone. Workplace safety is reinforced by consideration of when life events can affect focus and performance.

It takes a lot of courage and vulnerability to tell others about problems and pain, yet no one can receive support, a hand on the back, or a hug without inviting people into the shadows to show care and compassion.

I've spent the past five years involved in a lawsuit over a workplace fatality which could have been prevented and never should have happened. A safe place to work feels like a basic human right, but it requires training, awareness, reinforcement, constant attention, full engagement, focus, and attention to detail. Please consider bringing love, care, and compassion into the safety conversation and hold a safe space for people to bring their whole life to work. While we cannot solve each other's personal problems, we can support safe work and well-being 100% of the time.

ACTIVATING LOVING LEADERSHIP FOR SAFEST SAFETY:

1. Encourage teams to build check-ins into the communication cadence. At Niaga, we hosted bi-weekly all-hands meetings where financial updates were shared, and two teams shared milestone progress, wins, learnings, and risks. At the end of each meeting, we asked all participants to be on screen to answer two questions with thumbs up, sideways, or down: 1) How are you feeling about work at this moment? 2) How are you feeling overall at this moment? Any teammate who

expressed a thumbs down received calls from my teammates and me to understand the situation and provide support.

2. Put one-on-one meetings on your monthly agenda. Every time will not be convenient for every person every time, but there's a lot of comfort in knowing space is held for connection and dialogue every single month and bi-weekly or weekly for anyone seeking more engagement. Thirty hours of every month has been committed to (sixty) thirty-minute meetings with teammates and coaches at Niaga, and teammates were teammates whether they were employees, contractors, coaches, part-time, full-time, or otherwise. The agenda for these meetings was very fluid and tailored to the individual's needs in the generous present moment. In one session, we might talk about life, children, vacations, or hobbies. Another day might bring problem-solving in an active project. Interpersonal dilemmas or big ideas for a strategic pivot could take the stage. In any case, I enjoyed being on the same team, feeling connected to the crew, and sharing this crazy thing called life on top of the crazy journey of disruptive innovation.

3. As colleagues, take chances and lean into vulnerable communication. It's quite scary sometimes to share personal situations and challenges, but this is not a weakness; it is remarkably courageous to care and share yourself. It is an act of self-love to ask for help and understanding, and we all deserve accommodation and support in times of need. Remember that your actions to prioritize your own safety and the health of the whole team could be the example someone else follows on their next difficult day.

3

A NEW KIND OF LOVE

"If you want to make a Dutch person uncomfortable, tell 'em you love 'em."

—ME

I've made a case for love in its most basic form: a way of being and living life from this simple yet powerful connecting frequency. Love as a force or glue of goodness that flows between people, places, and things. Love as a bottomless, abundant, and expanding force that cannot be created or destroyed. It's always there, like the air we breathe. Our capacity to feel it, enjoy it, share it, and spread it is activated by our awareness of it.

I worked in the Netherlands from January of 2018 through May of 2023. This was an incredible period of my life for many reasons, and the things I learned and observed about Dutch culture were stimulating, impactful, and eye-opeining, especially since they could be compared and contrasted with (or were so different from) my experiences as a child of the United States. My passports were already full of stamps, and I'd logged millions of miles working with teams around the world, but there's simply nothing like the immersion of working on another continent and in another country. I'd love to do it again and again! I've already placed an order with the universe to learn ten to fifteen languages in my next lifetime.

While I resist stereotypes, a few things were remarkably consistent as I experienced Dutch people and their culture. First, many Dutch people are very modest and humble. They are not used to being recognized or celebrated, and my American expressions of gratitude or appreciation—especially out loud, in public—were met with discomfort and a step aside, as if they channeled Keanu Reeves in *The Matrix* and could deep-bend to avoid being hit by the energy. I went so far as to host a Gratitude Dinner one year, surveying the group and asking each colleague to recognize the contributions and strengths of three other teammates. I used the input to create framed gifts for each person (thanks, Bill Podojil, for this example) and placed them around the room. Some frames were big, recognizing ten to twelve pieces of feedback, and others were small, with only one to two notes. At each place setting, two Niaga 'Gifts of Gratitude' certificates were waiting to be filled out. Between courses, I would make a choice like, "*Look at the person two seats to your left and take three minutes to write something you admire or appreciate about them.*" Then, during that course, each person would stand up, address the person they would share the compliment with, and then hand them the little card. These little 'awards' were easy when we knew the person well and more difficult with a stranger. Yet, when we try, it's quite easy to see something worth noting in anyone.

This dinner was lovely, loving, and a great experience for most, but it did take most of the group WAAAYYY out of their comfort zones. I learned quickly that Dutch kids are raised to deeply value equality and to tolerate others even if you don't like them. No one is special, and they learn to keep their heads in line with everyone else. This contrasts the American Dream, where anyone can be anything, where great wealth and celebrity are possible for all, if achieved by only a few.

The good news: We openly discussed these tensions, norms, preferences, and values together. Over time, the team embraced the crazy ways we planned our work, worked our plans, and paused to play together. I adapted to their comfort, stretch, and panic zones while remaining true to myself. From time to time, I did tell them I loved them, the partnerships they built, and the courage shown by owning setbacks on difficult days. Only a few people ever said it back, and yet I knew the energy flowed as love does in our dynamic team, proving circular economy business models and practices.

We each get to experience and define love in any way that serves us and our relationships with ourselves, each other, and the world. I'm asking, though, that we all pause and consider the value of embracing love as abundant, important, and always best when flowing freely. Any resistance or restrictions to love, as the most powerful frequency and connecting energy in the world, simply hold us back from our true selves, better relationships, and better outcomes for all.

Let's talk about love. Let's balance all seven essential energies: connection, creation, emotion, love, free will, insight, and consciousness to bring the best of our human nature to our lives and into our work.

After years of societal stories about powerful leadership favoring—if not requiring—stoicism, hierarchy, competition, force, and silos, I'm here to challenge the bias that there's no place for love at work. I challenge everyone to show me how the highest levels of collaboration, inclusion, empowerment, and effectiveness can be achieved without welcoming and activating the feminine side of every human's whole self: It takes care, nurture, kindness, compassion, and love in all of us to reach peak levels of trust, confidence, and performance.

Activating love at work starts with the self. Take some time to assess your relationship with love, with your heart, and how you experience the love in your life. Assess the flow of goodness, openness, and trust in every relationship in your life. Where things are smooth, effortless, consistent, and always good, ask why.

Where things are pinched off, regulated, restricted, or soaking in judgment, separation, power dynamics, or pain, ask why. I promise you it's entirely possible to eliminate the dis-ease (friction, fear, worry, shame, blame, anger, resentment...) in every relationship we have, from our relationship to our self, our bodies, our families, our friends, and our co-workers. This is the most rewarding, restoring, inspiring, and empowering work we can do in our lives.

I invite you to join me in the shifts and resets that could possibly change the world for generations to come and rebalance planet Earth. All the innovation, recycling, climate action, and medicine in the world will never have the impact of eight billion people unifying in love, kindness, and conscious capitalism together.

4

LEAN INTO LOVE

"Catch people doing something right [and celebrate them]."

—KEN BLANCHARD

What does it mean to bring love to work? While the word love is not prominent in most factories, offices, or conference rooms, it is easy to observe loving behaviors and loving energy all day long. Even in the most toxic cultures, individuals and departments often flourish where even one individual affects the local/microclimate by fostering engagement, empowerment, and trust.

Expressing love simply means connecting with care, compassion, concern, curiosity, and kindness. It means holding space for understanding, exploration, and creation with your greatest good, my greatest good, and the collective greatest good in heart and mind. I'm confident plenty of love flows and flourishes in your company and your life. Just imagine how much more is possible with your awareness and intention, and then everyone's activation in time! As you read the list below, how many of these things are already normal for you or easily observed in your work culture?

18 WAYS TO BRING LOVE TO WORK:

1. Keep the most important thing the most important thing. In my experience, deep alignment of purpose and mission is critical to attract and empower top talent. When all players in the ecosystem share an urgent pursuit of the mission and a personal connection to the desired future state, the stage is set for creation and delivery. When the reason for the organization's existence and contribution to the world are crystal clear, activating the highest-performing team becomes the daily work.

2. Greet people in passing, whether offering a 'good morning' or eye contact with a smile or a nod. Some people are good at a friendly handshake or arm touch, while others are more reserved. I vividly remember complaints about an executive at one of my jobs who always took the stairs for exercise, but when meeting people in the stairwell he was either absorbed in his phone or bounding two steps at a time with his head down.

3. MBWA: Management by walking around. Step away from your desk and schedule time to connect with colleagues. Enjoy the time at the coffee pot or the ten minutes before a meeting starts to check in and catch up. If you're working remotely, get creative about connecting beyond the topic at hand.

4. Learn and remember names. Address people by their names, exactly as they pronounce their names. If you don't know or can't remember, ask again and try harder. I went to a training where we had to look a person in the face and say, "I'm sorry, but I don't care enough about you to remember your name." Believe me, you only

have to go through this one time to realize that a) it's not that hard, and b) it means a lot when people see, know, and remember us.

5. Be impeccable with time. Show respect for all participants in every scheduled activity by treasuring their time. If you are going to be late, communicate ahead of time and reschedule proactively. If tardiness is a habit you need to break, create a consequence. Ten dollars for every five-minute delay can fund a nice happy hour for the team.

6. Give feedback as close to the moment as possible. The most valuable feedback you can give is reinforcing strengths and catching people doing things right. The second-most valuable feedback is straight talk when something isn't going well. Peer feedback is a skill worth building, as we spend a lot more time working with teammates than being directly observed by a supervisor. Small adjustments can pay big dividends when it is safe, and even comfortable, to share insights and observations about behaviors and actions that affect each other and the team.

7. Ask questions! We already know what we know about everything, so suspending our current beliefs and opinions to genuinely understand what someone else sees and feels is the easiest way to find any common ground. Those of us who are very comfortable with our intuition and "facts" may unknowingly stand in the way of something even better, easier, more efficient, or lower risk.

8. Put time into performance and development conversations and hold them frequently. As an employee, be the CEO of your own life and ask for time to discuss progress, performance, and skill-building if the time isn't magically appearing in your calendar. As a team leader, supervisor, or executive, block time to think about the team

and individual contributions. Prepare for these important sessions and invest in the team as you would like someone to invest in you.

9. Celebrate achievements and milestones. From safety records to service milestones, delivering innovations to owning a failure, pause to see and call out big and small wins. Using communication programs to recognize personal events, like birthdays, weddings, births, and graduations, shows that we care about each other's whole lives.

10. Treat everyone as adults. We often experience hierarchy in a parent-child, teacher-student, or boss-worker relationship with conscious and unconscious subordination. A little shift from leader-as-boss to leader-as-coach separates responsibilities without implying subordination. The best coaches are not the best players, and the best players are not the best coaches—but a great coach can make the most of a top-talent team, and great teammates treasure a coach with the best playbook and capacity to get more from the group than the individuals.

11. Embrace hybrid work. So many of us are still sifting and sorting out the optimal way to work and the future of work after COVID-19 protocols ended. We have learned that we can trust people to work from home, and plenty of tools enable productivity and connection. At the same time, there is great value to physical presence and sharing office time. Teams, Zoom, and Hangouts are great, but there is a different dynamic when we sit together with stacks of Post-It notes and dedicated time for planning, organizing, and executing. Teammates should discuss and debate the best configuration and approach to their specific work and responsibilities. Owners and executives can only understand the balance that best fits their objectives and workforce by exploring the options and engaging in

dialogue. It is loving to care about the team's whole existence so members can feel supported as workers, parents, individuals, and friends with dynamic lives and competing priorities to balance.

12. Hold people responsible for outcomes, not hours. There have been times in my life when I've been super productive and could accomplish a week's worth of work in two days, and other times when I revisit a presentation twenty-five times, chewing up eighty hours in a single week. I've also known colleagues who delivered remarkable contributions in four-day weeks while others were social during the day and grinded out their work at night. When targets, milestones, and expectations are clear, and people are trusted to do the right thing and consistently deliver as promised, empower them to design their days and their lives in a way that fits their priorities and preferences.

13. Put the phones down. Across generations, we have become addicted to our smartphones, tablets, and laptops. These are magnificent tools, but they are no replacement for human connection. Care about each other enough to use spaces between meetings and events to say hello, reconnect, and catch up. You never know when that simple story shared at 10:55 a.m. will lead to common ground, a new opportunity, or a time-saving solution.

14. Focus on what you DO want, not what you DON'T want. There are plenty of books and coaches teaching the laws of attraction. On the most basic level, thoughts do become things, and words carry energy. If our language is sending signals of bad outcomes, don't be surprised when more of them appear. When we signal the desired outcome, natural forces support the path to it. As an example, Firm A might promote a zero-accident target, while Firm B might pro-

mote a perfectly safe workplace. Focusing energy on eliminating accidents is likely to facilitate more accidents than focusing energy on creating safety. Ending the drug war has largely failed. Prioritizing mental health, a basic quality of life for all, and safe drug consumption would probably get us a lot closer to a healthier society.

15. Be an anti-racist. Listen for examples of stereotypes and biases everywhere you go and become a skeptic of generalizations and assumptions based on any form of separation. Everyone has positive and negative behaviors and habits, just as we know ourselves to be. All X people are not Y way... ever. Stereotypes are never absolutes. Take the time to become a student and skeptic of your own programs, and encourage dialogue to learn about others' preferences, traditions, fears, and challenges. The more time we take to hear our own programs and to rewrite our "truths," the faster we include everything in this crazy, wonderful thing called life.

16. Teams who play together stay together. Build fun and casual connections into cycles at work. There's nothing better than sharing laughter, an adventure, or a surprise to connect colleagues and teams, and the best execution of social activities usually comes from the team itself. I've ridden bicycles across my home state with fifteen colleagues and hosted a pajama party movie night with thirty teammates on bean bags. It's as easy as forming a committee with a small budget and the freedom to surprise others. These memories will be cherished long after the work is done!

17. Make recognition memorable. As a young finance manager, I supported Margaret Dano, a global operations and supply chain executive. She was the master of impossible challenges, and yet when those lofty goals were met, our next leadership offsite was held at

a great location with the perfect combination of work and play. I was most touched, though, by the cards I would find on my desk after a sprint of above-and-beyond effort: Margaret would place a greeting card with a personal note and a crisp $50 or $100 bill, encouraging a little celebration like a happy hour or dinner date on her. This personal touch and splash of unexpected generosity have never been forgotten. I enjoy repeating this practice regularly.

18. Cancel autopilot to anticipate, expect, and allow growth. When we know people well, we cast their role in our own life movie and expect them to show up today as the same person we knew yesterday. We expect to see the same behaviors, beliefs, personalities, and values we've always held as truth. When we live on autopilot, we believe we know how people will behave because we subconsciously project what we expect. And yet, people are always shifting, growing, and changing. Core values may remain consistent, but anyone can change with new information and motivation. Can we honor and hold the space for people to learn and evolve? All it takes is checking in from time to time to see if a person is where you last left them or if they're in a different place now. Rinse and repeat.

How do you care, connect, and converse at work? It would be fun to expand this list to 100 Ways to Bring Your Love to Work, so please share ideas and best practices at loveworks.world!

5

EXPAND ABUNDANCE

"Abundance is not a result you create. It is an existing state you recognize."

—RALPH WALDO EMERSON

Have you ever seen the movie *In Time,* starring Justin Timberlake? SPOILER ALERT: Do not proceed if you'd like to watch it!

In Time is about a future where everyone has a chip installed in their arm, activated on your twenty-fifth birthday. From then on, you work for more time and spend time instead of money. You use time to live and pay for rent, food, etc. When you run out of time, you die. In communities where time is scarce, it's a race against the clock to gather time just to stay alive. When you have a sick or struggling loved one who can't gather more time, you work twice as hard to earn extra time to keep them alive. The people living in scarcity come to learn that other people have figured out how to bank their time, and they hold many lifetimes in the bank. While there is enough time for everyone in total, small groups are holding massive amounts of time while others drop dead all over the place every day.

Earth has ample resources to support all life on it. What would it take to ensure that every man, woman, and child has access to basic food, clothing, and safe shelter?

Each of us has a personal relationship with time, work, and money. I hope we can align on three things to start this conversation: First, our **lifetime** is finite—there is an expiration date for everyone. Second, it's hard to enjoy time or have money if you don't participate in work or creation of some kind. Third, money isn't very useful when we're dead. Can we agree to these basics in a discussion about abundance?

I see a world out of balance yet flowing with natural materials, vibrant energy, shared knowledge, and expanding innovation. There's plenty for everyone, yet more people drop into the shadows and struggle with each passing day.

Governments hold the capacity to shape systems providing a basic quality of life for all, but citizens resist taxation and regulation when the use of funds lacks transparency and unclear impacts erode trust. Some countries seem to get a basic 'quality of life' better than others, with tradeoffs between rights, freedoms, requirements, and rules. Massive amounts of money controlled by a few can come with corruption, favoritism, and protection of interests, OR it can ensure fertile ground for great things to flourish for all.

Few cocktail conversations are more polarizing than wealth redistribution, welfare, and socialism. (Unless you prefer to talk about religion, racism, and politics.) Any human likely desires a better world for themselves and for all, but carving up one limited pie of anything differently is bound to touch nerves and incite fear. No one wants to have less tomorrow than they have today, whether we're talking about health, wealth, relationships, or joy. That said, plenty of people would like to have less hunger, depression, anxiety, fear, and debt.

Capitalism is the force that can change the landscape faster than anything else! While some level of general taxation is needed to support infrastructure for advanced societies, we don't have to take more and more from the most affluent people to give it to others. We simply need to ask people with vast resources to welcome the rest of humanity to the party. By enrolling every human in participation, we can create a higher quality of life for every person, every family, and every community.

Of course, sick, disabled, and elderly humans will always require care and support to maintain a basic quality of life. What would you need if you were dis-eased and unable to work, and who would you expect that support to come from in the best version of the world? I would expect my family to support me—and be able to support me—first. Then, my community and country, through social welfare actions. With that said, there would be a lot fewer sick and dis-eased people if participation, education, community, healthy food, and financial stability were abundant!

Let's start to measure our impact differently. Instead of comparing net worth, let's compare net creation and net activation. As a leader, owner, or investor, how many families were employed in our care? How many degrees were earned in our enterprise? How much rent was paid? How much health was protected? How much did communities thrive while we were in town? How many charities provided services through our generosity? How many vacations were taken and memories collected because of the abundance we activated through our businesses and organizations?

As workers, we can also affect positive change in our communities. More restaurants and venues will employ more chefs, servers, and artists when we support local businesses by attending a performance or dining out. When we volunteer our time, we can help feed our communities, build affordable housing, provide companionship, and share our gifts. When we bring our best to work and love our projects, colleagues, and mission, we secure our place on the team. When the organization succeeds, new positions are created to support growth, and abundance expands again.

In the past year, I have used my abundance to travel, attend events, and decorate my new home with beautiful things. I attend retreats and enjoy self-care. I've also sent financial grants to organizations to fund harm reduction via psychedelic therapies, support cancer charities, give back to my university, advance mind-body connection research, secure clean water in Guatemala, and introduce kids to rodeo programs. I have been blessed with abundance through a great career, and I would like to use the rest of my lifetime helping as many people as possible find a way out of fear and scarcity and into enjoying this plentiful world and precious life. Could we do this together?

IDEAS TO ACTIVATE ABUNDANCE IN LOVING ORGANIZATIONS:

1. Encourage and celebrate charitable work happening throughout your company, at the enterprise level, or through individual recognition. I've worked for companies that built playgrounds as a team-building activity, enabled volunteer days as part of the annual calendar, and used payroll deductions to support United Way. Matching contributions supported individual giving. Holiday periods came with adopt a child or adopt a family gift or food drives.
2. Study the communities where we have operations. What is happening around the plant or office? What challenges are most pressing

in Marshalltown, perhaps different from Fargo or Greenville? How does our mission benefit the communities that serve us with talent and time? Does the enduring impact of planned changes have a net positive or negative impact on the families that have shared their lives with us? If there is a food desert in local communities following plant closures by peer companies, can we use our network and relationships to activate local entrepreneurs or bring an express grocer to town? If affordable housing is only available to hourly wage workers an hour away, solve that with effortless, inexpensive transportation or by affecting housing or wages in some way.

3. Prioritize participation over maximum shareholder returns, especially when facing decisions around restructuring, layoffs, and closures that are purely profit-motivated. Burning platforms and distressed situations call for change to protect the viability of a business, but where businesses are generating great returns, reach for inclusion and activation over the biggest bonuses for a few. Executives and owners should enjoy great abundance, and it's sweetest when everyone is thriving.

6

THE PINNACLE OF OUR POWER

"Good decisions come with wisdom, and wisdom comes from bad decisions."

—UNKNOWN

On New Year's Eve 2023, eight guests and their children each shared what we were most thankful for as we enjoyed a traditional feast around my dinner table and welcomed the new year. My friend, Sean Kennedy, expressed gratitude for this time in his life when he said "... I am at **the Pinnacle of My Power."** Over the course of sixty birthdays, Sean had accumulated treasured relationships, a great education, many adventures, and a vibrant career. Aware of his good fortune and his well-functioning body and mind, Sean held and owned an overflowing capacity to leverage his lifetime of learning, pursue his passions, and give back to others in need. The rest of us sat in silence for a moment as we absorbed this refreshing perspective.

Sean is full of energy, and his passions for climate action, kilowatts, and sunshine feel like a perfect fit. When he's not in Washington, D.C. or Iowa pursuing solar projects, you'll find him in Ukraine learning the language, working on energy restoration, or helping repair bomb-damaged homes by replacing windows and roofs. Let's not forget Sean's extracurricular activities as a beekeeper with a bee rescue program. Sean teaches and mentors others to protect our bee population, retrieving swarms from buildings and trees and returning them safely to the Swiss Embassy property hives. The vacuum packs combined with beekeeping gear are bound to make you think the Ghostbusters have arrived! He is a great example of living an authentic life to its fullest.

In the following days, I pondered this idea of the Pinnacle of Our Power and realized that we are never more talented, educated, informed, experienced, or capable than we are right now, in this present moment.

Whether we are twenty-five or seventy-five, on any given day, we have all the education, skills, and experiences we're going to have that day until we pick up this day's experiences, challenges, and news to learn something new. Every unfolding day, we can leverage what we know and pivot when it's time to forge a new direction into tomorrow. There will always be skills to acquire and knowledge to gain to be competent in new assignments, but the pursuit of learning and mastery is the game of life. No one said life would be *easy*—they said the journey full of twists and turns would be *worth it*!

If we could embrace that each of us is perfectly complete with everything life has presented to us so far, and we are individually as good as we can be for today, an opportunity appears to maximize the value we can get from participating in this day, all day long.

Let's consider the amount of energy—in human potential—alive in any space. When we are in line with ten people before a presentation, speech, concert, or big game, there are nine peers with a heartbeat, sharing the same air, experiencing the same passing time. Behold the energy when ten people are excited, anticipating intrigue or pleasure, and having the time of their lives. Then, consider the energy when ten people face change, witness an accident, share an awkward moment after an inappropriate joke, or face any inequity. There's an observable 'wobble' introduced when people are not equally safe or sharing a mission or purpose. This only intensifies when power dynamics or dis-ease are present; add fear, anxiety, frustration, or distrust to any group, and the 'wobble' amplifies, gaining strength.

We've all witnessed the shift when a group's collective energy is tapped and unleashed on a great opportunity or impossible challenge. Humans have sent each other to the moon and the International Space Station through collaboration, problem-solving, learning from failures, and relentlessly pursuing breakthroughs. Every time a group of musicians comes together to form a band, each individual's talent and skill complements another to create harmony, rhythm, and—dare I say—*magic*. When artists perform well, we share the experience, compelled to listen, sing along. and dance. I'm equally drawn to the talented kids on TikTok showcasing their gifts, a street drummer playing five-gallon buckets, a marching band at a parade, and celebrities performing in a fifty-year reunion tour. We all know how it feels to be in the presence of people sharing their talents and gifts, doing something they love, and growing in competence, capability, and results right in front of our eyes.

What energy could we unleash in every workforce if we saw all the experience, knowledge, capacity, and capability held in each body and mind? What could we do with the constant pinnacle of our individual and collective power when we expect each other to be capable of whatever we apply ourselves to?

What would happen if we put even more care into matching ourselves and our teammates with roles and responsibilities that deeply align with our strengths, interests, and motivations? What would happen if we embraced master-and-apprentice examples to pair learners with teachers for accelerated, hands-on knowledge transfer and rapid development? When do we get to be honest about jobs that don't fit and dreams that are unfulfilled so more of us get to use our lifetime to create meaningful impact, joy, and financial security?

As I pondered the possibilities, my favorite interview questions came to mind. When I'm exploring interested and interesting candidates for jobs, I frequently turn the resume over and ask the person two sets of questions: A) When were you having the most fun and experiencing a great fit with your skills and interests? Have you experienced a time when you were so excited about the work that you couldn't stop thinking about the project and would have done the work for free? B) On the flip side, have you experienced a role or assignments that were not a great fit, and took unusual effort or initiative to complete the assignment or projects? In other words, have you had enough diversity in your work to also know what you don't like to do or what takes more effort and energy than it should?

My own answer to this question is not tied to any of the jobs on my resume or achievements teams have delivered in our time together. It is rooted in a parallel life experience, which I brought to work along the way.

When I had cancer the first time, the end of my treatment plan came with a recommendation to take a drug called Tamoxifen for as many as ten years. My body did not tolerate the medication well as it forced my forty-year-old body into menopause. The hot flashes were particularly awful, soaking the sheets and keeping me awake at night. On airplanes and trains, I'd be so physically uncomfortable burning up in my suits and heels, I wanted to peel my skin off to find some relief. I made a personal decision to stop taking the medication against three doctors' recommendations.

Desperate for alternatives, I took a crash course in nutrition, reading many books and watching documentaries about how plant-centric diets have reversed heart disease, diabetes, and some cancers. I went to seminars and hired personal chefs to cook for our family while we were at work and school, coming home to fresh and healthy plant-based food in the refrigerator twice a week. I adopted a strict diet of vegetables, fruits, beans, and grains while minimizing alcohol, caffeine, and sugars. In a very short time, I had more energy than ever and felt amazing.

Miraculously, in just months, every single health issue I'd ever had, from benign thyroid cysts to adult acne, resolved naturally.

There's a joke which asks, "How do you know when someone is a vegan? Just wait five minutes, and they'll tell you." I enjoyed talking to people who reacted to the things I ordered at restaurants or the food I ate for lunch at work, but also quickly learned not to judge what others put on their plates. Nutrition is a personal freedom, and my husband was one of the loudest voices when it came to the soapbox I stepped onto from time to time. I quickly learned to enjoy my choices and excellent health while appreciating that everyone gets to choose what they eat and drink.

At the office, I observed colleagues facing health challenges, but I prioritized respect for each person's choices and preferences in their own lives. Sharing my experiences and knowledge about food and disease didn't feel important. This changed, though, with an upsetting phone call on Saturday, January 25, 2015. I was at the NFL Pro Bowl in Glendale, Arizona, when Anita Sturtz, our Director of Customer Service, called to share terrible news.

One of our colleagues had died of a heart attack that morning—a fifty-two-year-old woman I'd chatted with just days before. Diane was a long-term employee with the customer service team, and beloved by her teammates and her customers. Her husband was also employed at

Avery Dennison, and their only son was well-known to the group. We were shocked and saddened by the news, and Anita and I had several conversations about how we could support the team and make a difference in their health and lives. After all, the work was stimulating but sedentary. We already had software on our computers to encourage stretch breaks, and workplace wellness programs encouraged everyone to move 10,000 steps/day. Could we possibly do more?

We discussed using the upcoming National Sales Meeting to broach the topic of healthy living while we were together. Anita and I were equally passionate about nourishment and lifestyle, and we thought it would be interesting to talk about these things at work.

In my "magic time" after hours and on weekends, I created a program called Fuel for Life. This thirty-day challenge involved adopting a plant-based diet to see how much our health and bodies changed in a short period of time. I created a presentation about disease and nutrition that was full of facts and information, and I started thinking about the safest way to test this initiative.

I knew firsthand that a person's body could change quickly, and I was worried about people with health conditions and medications. Wanting to put safety first, I called Dr. Caldwell Esselstyn, who worked at the Cleveland Clinic. I knew of him through the book *How to Prevent and Reverse Heart Disease* and the movie *Forks over Knives*. His wife and daughter had created a fantastic cookbook full of recipes that complemented his book and research. I only wanted someone from his staff to guide me on keeping people safe.

The same day I sent the email, my phone rang, and it was Dr. Esselstyn calling. I was so excited and overwhelmed that it might as well have been Bradley Cooper on the line. He personally responded to my message out of curiosity and his own unmet need in the world. In research twenty years prior and with thousands since, Dr. Esselstyn has proven the successful and consistent reversal of severe heart disease with diet and lifestyle alone. He tried to change the course of treatment at the Cleveland Clinic, where hearts, brains, and bones are profitable disciplines in the medical system. He also tried to change regulations and food guidelines only to find the FDA was highly influenced by the processed food industry. He was also aware that 110 million Americans received their medical insurance through self-insured corporations—the same companies that could directly benefit from healthier and more productive employees through lower medical costs and premiums, let alone fewer sick days.

Dr. Esselstyn agreed to support my program for a minimal cost and hoped we could learn together. He helped us with HIPAA compliance, on-site teams to draw blood and capture biometrics, and a special arrangement with the Cleveland Heart Lab to analyze the blood samples on day 1 and day 30. I would only receive the aggregated results for the program participants, and he would personally advise anyone who wanted to understand their own results and changes.

In addition to organizing Dr. Esselstyn's presentation, finding the supplier for biometrics and blood tests on-site, and gathering the materials to register and track participants, I purchased books, DVDs, and cookbooks to put on every floor of the office. I collaborated with the supplier for our workplace cafeteria, negotiating with them to add a plant-based entrée to the daily menu in sufficient quantities for people to take meals home for dinner. Our team coordinator, Rachel, scheduled a weekly 'Talk-O' Tuesday video conference to share experiences and ask questions, making it less lonely in the early weeks when caffeine withdrawals, cravings, and bloating can make 'hangry' seem mild. We organized potluck lunches on Fridays to taste a wide variety of foods prepared at home without meat, eggs, dairy, or oils. Rachel created a Google Drive folder where people could share recipes and photos, and I still make some of these recipes to this day.

I sought support to proceed, knowing nothing bad would happen as people ate more vegetables at every meal and great improvements in health could be experienced in a matter of weeks. My boss, who led our division, encouraged the initiative as his parents had struggled with cancer recently.

Even with his support, though, the introduction of the program was met with calls to the corporate ethics hotline. I was accused of abusing my positional power to make people change their diets, and lawyers encouraged me to stand down. I listened but took a personal position at my own risk, knowing I would never stop helping fifty people because two or three didn't like it or agree with me.

We implemented the program with fifty people who signed up for the blood work and biometrics of their own free will and with their own money. Dr. Esselstyn was the keynote speaker at our sales meeting, addressing 200 colleagues, and we took workplace wellness past wearing pedometers and counting steps and into our kitchens and digestive systems. The results were utterly incredible, and one testimonial after another told stories of transformations for the program participants and their loved ones at home. The potlucks and conference calls brought people together in community and dialogue, and we shared recipes, experiences, and positive change at work. We ran the program two times, and while I don't believe many people adopted a vegan lifestyle, I'm quite certain there is a heck of a lot more vegetables at every meal based on everything we learned together.

This was one of the most stimulating, rewarding, and fun things I've done in my life, and to this day, eight-plus years later, I still receive emails about the impact this experience had on lives and families. I created this from my heart, out of a love for health and nutrition and a love for the people I worked with every single day.

When our personal passions meet our strengths to serve others, the hard work is a pleasure, and the outcomes are not only achieved but paid forward as changes stick and grow.

I almost executed a pivot to turn Fuel for Life into a chain of plant-based kitchens, hoping to make it as easy to get delicious, healthy, plant-based foods as it is to get a sub sandwich or burger. The business plan was well on its way before other opportunities found me, and I went to the Netherlands to work with Niaga on entrepreneurship. I was counting my blessings in 2020 when COVID-19 closed one business after another, but to this day, I revisit that business plan from time to time. You never know!

We all know what it's like when something happens *to us* instead of *with us*. The child inside of ourselves revisits sitting at the kitchen table, facing the pile of broccoli or brussels sprouts we had to eat before being excused. It was miserable compared to the days our favorite meal was on the table, and we kept our membership in the Clean Plate Club, devouring every bite with gratitude and bliss.

We are at the Pinnacle of Our Power as humans when our skills, strengths, and passions are aligned with our work and at the tip-top of the summit when that work is in service to others. It is also very powerful to hold a vision for our legacy, using our investment in professions, projects, and creations to affect others, communities, and the world for generations to come.

SUGGESTIONS FOR LOVING LEADERSHIP ACTIVATION:

1. As Loving Leaders, we take great care to know the interests, experiences, and drivers for ourselves and our teammates. We do our best to match our talents with roles and responsibilities where we'll thrive and learn, and we seek stretch assignments along the way. It's more than fine to develop in our stretch zones, with a hand on each other's backs to encourage risk-taking, to allow discomfort and the stress that comes with the unknown or trying something that we haven't done before.
2. What is your answer to the activities and environments where you flourish as a leader and contributor? Are you aware of the tasks and responsibilities that drain your energy and take the most from you? Are there people around you who are strong where you are weak or shine in circumstances that test you?
3. Agile work groups that utilize sprints to organize work frequently leverage retrospectives at the end of each period, taking a pause to reflect on how the work is being done and what can be improved in the next phase. Use this time to reflect on what each person enjoys and is stimulated by and what is particularly difficult or draining. Adapt where needed to match tasks and deliverables with strengths or learning zones to develop skills and abilities intentionally.
4. Make time for mentorship and networking: Everyone can benefit from exposure to people in different stages of careers, from different backgrounds, educations, and departments. It takes a little courage and a small investment in time to ask for someone's time

and help, but something as simple as a bi-monthly coffee with a leader you admire or a peer you're impressed by can go a long way to open doors and build networks. If you're curious about a different department, ask to shadow someone for an hour or a day. If you've never met a customer, ride along with a rep. On the flip side, if there is a problem to solve or an idea to explore, host a potluck lunch or roundtable dialogue with the most diverse group you can find for an hour. Present the situation and then listen to the discussion like a fly on the wall. Gather insights and ideas and share any helpful perspectives or actions that come from team time.

7

ON PURPOSE, WITH PURPOSE

"The magic is not in what we do, but in why we do it."

—SIMON SINEK

I've been very fortunate to work with many great teams and with many wonderful and talented people throughout my career. I embraced the mission and purpose in every organization as if it were my own. I've fallen in love with Peruvian farmers growing coffee organically so that we can import, roast, and distribute it to the lovely owners of natural food grocers and cooperatives in the U.S. I've been a proud steward of brands from GlueStic and Avery to CleanFlake and Canary. I've defended prices and value in bids and tenders, hosted customer councils, and consumed coffee and conversation at trade shows with pleasure. My colleagues and customers have become my friends, and work has always felt like a home away from home to me.

I'll never forget my first date with my second husband. (For the record, there are only two... so far.) I'd been on a string of dead-end introductions, so I was skeptical of another blind date or match through It's Just Lunch. It was a pleasant surprise when I arrived to find a tall, handsome man who looked like he'd walked off a *GQ* cover. He was looking at me with kind eyes, a warm smile, and was well-dressed from crown to toe. My head was in the clouds while I ordered a glass of wine and prepared for a complete waste of time. In my mind, he was never going to be interested in me.

Gary asked me what I did for a living, and I told him my truth: "I save lives."

"Hmm… how do you save lives?" he asked.

"I lead a team that designs and manufactures the glass bead and prismatic films that become road signs. We help drivers around the world reach their destinations safely," I answered, then countered, "So what do you do with your time and talent?"

"I really save lives."

"Tell me more," I said, intrigued.

"I was a nurse manager in the cardiovascular surgery unit of the Cleveland Clinic, and now I sell a medical device that restores blood flow to peripheral arteries."

He won!

I've found it easy to understand, feel, and adopt the mission and purpose of every company I've ever worked for—a testament to each firm's ability to articulate an intention and bring it to life. My enthusiasm for the WHY behind the work was tied to the connection I felt to the cause and the people sharing the journey. Collectively, we were contributing to something important, impactful, and good.

With that said, nothing has been even close to how it felt to be part of the Niaga team. This diverse group of inventors, chemists, engineers, marketeers, controllers, cultural anthropologists, operators, service professionals, coaches, and more brought an entirely new level to meaningful, purpose-driven work. With Niaga as the word 'again' spelled backward, we shared a purpose to 'Design to Use Again.' The entire sentence should read: We were out to eliminate the top bulky waste issues in the world—carpets and rugs, mattresses and furniture. Sadly, >97% of these items end up in landfills and incinerators around the world today.

In addition to designing recyclable products, we aimed to utilize closed-loop systems and recycling techniques to recover, reuse, and recycle all materials.

This team hungered for a better world and showed remarkable resilience and conviction through disruptive innovation's inevitable highs and lows. We live in a world that resists change and protects the status quo with ferocity. New materials and new methods that cost more or reduce productivity and profitability before reaching scale are remarkably hard to sell and adopt—no matter how big the future impact can be or how awful the current state truly is for people or the planet. Add the pressure and anxiety that come with the pre-profit years, where millions are spent to test concepts, prove technologies, and win the first customers. It's damn hard to sustain a top-talent team through the rollercoaster ride of risk, trials, failures, and breakthroughs even before you add a pandemic and changing owners to the venture.

The Niaga team members were purpose-driven, but we did not have the same individual 'whys' that drove our inspiration and engagement. The founder of Niaga was deeply frustrated by the waste in the world, and he lost sleep at night over the precious raw materials that were being used one time and ending up as trash. He owned the patents for a new production method to make carpet out of one material instead of fifteen—a material that could be recovered, recycled, and reused again and again. Other teammates were bushwhackers and environmentalists who cared about nature and protecting the land and the earth's beauty and resources. Some people were passionate about the oceans and deeply concerned about plastic contamination, endangered and extinct species, and water quality.

As a cancer survivor, I cared most about health, eliminating toxic materials, and improving indoor air quality. We were all on the same business team, sharing the Niaga dream, planning the work, and working the plans, but the sum of the individual passions driving momentum, intense focus on milestone delivery, pursuing like-minded partners, and proving the impossible was much bigger than the Niaga mission alone. It was infectious, inspiring, and powerfully important as we gathered to march uphill every single day.

LOVING LEADERSHIP ACTIVATION:

1. How clear and compelling is the purpose and mission of the company's work? Can you feel the collective connection to the importance of what you do, sell, provide, or create? Hold retrospective sessions with a few focus groups representing cross-functional and diverse teammates throughout the enterprise and listen to what colleagues have to say. How do teammates describe the company's purpose on a plane or at a family reunion? Is the mission and purpose important to the world and to you personally? How could we use the company's assets, product lines, service portfolio, or teams to have a bigger, better, or broader positive impact for our clients, communities, and the world? Is there anything our stakeholders don't like or appreciate about our company's work or impact today?
2. Do we know why each teammate comes to work? Is anyone punch-

ing the clock out of a basic need for food, housing, clothing, and survival? Does each lady or gentleman connect to the reason the firm exists? Do we feel our work is important, and understand how every role is essential in the total capability to do what we do? Connecting the individual whys to the collective purpose is a wonderful way to build loyalty, care for quality, and bank emotional capital for when it's time to ask for the extra mile. Can we love our work, love each other, love our customers, love our products and services, and love to serve? I'll bet on the leaders that activate the most love, connection, and commitment to delivering with and for each other and the world every time.

8

COMMANDER TO COACH

"We are greater than, and greater for, the sum of us."

—HEATHER McGHEE

For twenty years, the first words that leave my mouth addressing a new business team or organization have been, "To the best of my ability, things will happen WITH YOU and not TO YOU."

Listen, I'll be completely honest: As someone working in very technical companies with no technical training, I was worthless if the right experts weren't at the table. When I accepted the role of general manager for Avery Dennison's Reflective Solutions team, I didn't know a thing about the retroreflective properties of glass bead and prismatic materials. I knew nothing about polyester, pyrolysis, or thermal dynamics when I joined the Niaga team. Thankfully, I was surrounded by people who did!

As a human, I've resisted being told what to do or how things are going to go, and I've loved being at the table for discussions, debates, and dialogue. The best plans and deepest execution have always followed the right skeptics asking very annoying questions and a new perspective from a peer with a very different point of view, leaving me with some combination of "A-HA" or "Holy [Cow]" when I didn't see that implication, possibility, or risk at all.

No matter how clearly or frequently I said this phrase, people didn't believe me. The skepticism naturally came from life-to-date experiences with work, conceptions of "management" as 'them versus me,' and normal work packages. Most workers are used to delegating tasks and goals for the year, broken down by quarter, and acknowledged in a written performance plan. As I shaped forums to bring colleagues together across functions and geographies to discuss priorities, choose the most important work, and shape culture and climate, three camps inevitably emerged:

- Those resistant to change
- Those grateful for the opportunity
- Those shocked you're interested in anything they have to say

First, a story of resistance.

My career aspiration in my twenties and thirties was to earn a coveted general manager role, run a discreet business with a cross-functional team, and be accountable for the financial performance of the division. As my corporation reorganized from a decentralized firm with many general managers running many regional businesses to four worldwide divisions in functional order, the GM roles became few and far between. Women in these roles were even more scarce, but there were a few, giving me reason to believe I could get there eventually. I was fortunate to have mentors who saw my potential and encouraged pursuing that dream. At the same time, I'd held many lateral director-level roles, so many I secretly wondered if I could compete for jobs at other companies. My resume was broad but not deep; how could I compete with someone focused on marketing, finance, operations, or sales their whole career?

Eventually, I was offered leadership of the company's smallest division, which was underperforming expectations in almost every way. Boston Consulting Group had just completed a study concluding our division would never successfully compete against the market share leader in the category: the worthy adversary called 3M. The playbook was designed and organized: Hire someone to reduce costs by closing one plant, 'fire' fifty-two unprofitable customers, and simplify to profitable product lines more aligned with the larger commercial graphics business.

I was thrilled to be chosen for this opportunity. In addition to finally receiving the promotion, I was going to work for Helen Saunders, a highly regarded female executive who had worked her way up from entry-level roles to the top ranks of our organization. She was bright, beautiful, and full of charisma from her toes to her crown, with a delightful British accent. I knew I could learn a lot from her business savvy and feminine force.

As I met the team and started learning the technology and product lines, the first order of business was organizing a meeting with commercial leaders around the globe and functional leaders in Cleveland and Chicago. In our time together, we would discuss the BCG study and action plans while exploring the team's thoughts on top value creation opportunities they saw as stakeholders in the business.

In the first months of this work, we absorbed product development ideas from Australia and Brazil that were applicable to other regions. We learned of infrastructure builds in China before the 2008 Summer Olympic Games and in India as the Golden Quadrilateral highway system was emerging. Data revealed portfolio complexity and production challenges. While there were hundreds of ideas in the funnel, as a team, we were on the hunt for the top ten priorities that could move the needle.

One of the "insights" from the BCG study recognized the low profitability of our long-term relationships with traffic sign converters in North America. 3M aggressively shaped standards that fit their portfolio and influenced governmental bids to identify testing protocols and specifications few others could meet. Their dominant market share extended globally in the retroreflective materials used in traffic signs, license plates, validation decal stickers, work zone safety products, and safety garments.

Our single-digit market share suggested sign makers and reflective product producers working with us wanted or needed an alternative to 3M. To this day, I believe our products met the standards set collaboratively via ISO and ASTM protocols and were superior in many ways. The top-tier consultants had concluded Avery had no business competing with 3M in the regulated traffic sign category, as 3M was the clear giant with ~80% market share globally. While I understood the case and landscape the fancy report had framed, I remained curious about the strongest #2 position we could take when government bids *required* competition. It was time to go listen to the customers on the "to be fired" list.

Honoring my "with you, not to you" promise, I crafted an email for the North American team to enroll them on a road trip to meet top accounts. I asked for opportunities to sit with each sales leader and the customer-owner or leadership to understand their mission and operations, how they viewed us, how well things worked between our firms, and where they saw opportunities to be better together.

In the worst case, we were going to be winding things down anyway. In the best case, we might learn something that creates value for everyone.

I pushed SEND and called it a day. The next morning, Scott, one of our very experienced sales professionals, returned my call with a very simple reply. It was brief—simply the three letters 'LMB.'

I was not familiar with the term 'LMB;' so I picked up the phone to ask another teammate, Mark, for clarification. "Hi, Mark. This is Kelly. I just received a message from Scott with just three letters. Would you happen to know what 'LMB' means?"

After an uncomfortable laugh, Mark shared that LMB stands for "Lick My Balls." Apparently, as a new leader invading Scott's important account and looking over his shoulder, I was not as welcome as I had hoped.

While my intent was to set a stage for high collaboration and inclusive dialogue, at least one person was holding his cards tightly against his chest.

Thank goodness the Iowa farm girl in me thought that was creative and funny. It was an accident that this email was returned to me when the intended recipients were Scott's friends on the team. I probably could have created a painful moment for Scott if I had used my position or relationship with HR to document the situation and capture the moment in his permanent record. Deep inside, I knew we would eventually see each other more clearly. It took a minute, but in time, we spent two weeks riding our bikes across Iowa together, and he's been at my family's breakfast table eating my mom's cinnamon rolls.

Shifting culture and bringing love to work will follow the same pattern as any change. Some of us will be early adopters, while some of us will wait and see. The actual experience over time always offers proof of positive or negative outcomes. The range of reactions to new ideas, practices, and policies is generally predictable, so lean into persistence, perseverance, and constant conversation to elevate connection, build trust, and get the love flowing.

Second, a story about uncomfortable chairs at a new table.

I started working at Niaga in January of 2018. This group of twenty was out to prove circular economies are possible and profitable. Niaga technology was compelling, the brand was cool, and colleagues were smart, creative, and committed. Sadly, though, people were frustrated with each other; one hundred projects were incomplete, and cash was burning. The first customer was activated but unhappy. The team was much better at selling a dream than monetizing IP licenses, materials, or equipment.

After spending time with as many teammates as possible and reviewing the venture's project deck and annual targets, I invited everyone to our first workshop. With seats for everyone in a conference room, seven to eight individuals looked comfortable, five to six seemed apprehensive yet curious, and the rest appeared beyond their comfort zone and skeptical. I introduced myself again and declared to the best of my ability that things would happen With You and Not to You. We used our time in those early days to reset the culture, sow seeds for higher trust, create a "Partnership for a Drama-Free Niaga" and whittle our one-hundred-deep project list down to three business-critical priorities.

In the first one hundred days, some people would not sign the "Drama-Free" partnership. For them, proof was required to believe the shitshow could evolve. Even with skepticism and healing wounds, the shared purpose held by the team to prove design for reuse and recycling down the road locked hearts to the journey and fanned the motivation to try something new. A love of the dream and a passion for the purpose enabled space to approach things differently. As we shaped three 'must-win' battles and faced relentless criticism from our only paying customer, it was imperative to connect and reconnect relationships to foster a new type of teamwork.

One of Niaga's pilot line operators spoke for his team, asking, "Why am I here? I run the line, and no one has ever asked for my opinion before. Everyone else here has a lot more to say about these topics than I ever will, and I would rather be in the hall." This courageous voice opened space for others who had the same questions and concerns. "I'm a lab technician. I'd be more comfortable simply focusing on my experiments." "I'm very busy writing communications and creating campaigns. I don't really have three days to carve out for your stuff."

I simply shared my belief that EVERYONE does better work when they understand the context they are working in. When we share a purpose and awareness of the goals and critical activities to deliver, any work in the system is aligned with WHY it's important, WHEN it's required, WHO will be responsible, HOW we're defining the path of least resistance, WHAT could go wrong, and WHERE we will be when we're successful in our mission. We all get to know who the customers are, and it will take all of us to attract their partnership, their business, and their money to pay our bills and fund our growth.

Over time, any Niaga teammate could comfortably discuss our priorities, structure, the path to profitability, and the next milestones. When we pivoted from a project or changed course, everyone had opportunities to ask questions and challenge decisions before they were final. It does take time and money to engage and enroll broader groups of people in plans and execution, but the payoff is alignment, context, and speed when knowledge and motivation are tuned in and turned on for the entire crew. It really didn't take long before team workshops, held three times each year, became forums we didn't want to miss.

Last is a story about sharing struggles.

Alwin was a chemist who worked in research and development for more than ten years. He had a passion for product design and innovation, always seeking to be on the bleeding edge of new ideas and novel solutions to big problems. He worked in a small office and lab space with close colleagues and was happy with his assignments, compensation, and teamwork. After two years with Niaga, Alwin was unsure of his fit with changing responsibilities. He was teetering on burnout with an expanding and ever-changing workload. He felt immense pressure to create miracles against all odds in this venture.

I had never heard of burnout as an American corporate citizen, and when I learned of Alwin's sudden leave of absence tied to an incapacitating anxiety over work, I asked my boss what the hell was going on. I quickly learned that 'burnout'' was recognized in the Netherlands as a critical mental and occupational health concern. Employees facing burnout are supported with a leave of absence, occupational therapy, medical support if required, and—if rehabilitated—a thoughtful and slow re-entry to limited and part-time work. The employee only returns to employment when ready.

Now, I was admittedly gobsmacked. I was a new resident of a country where it's normal to enter the workforce with five weeks of vacation per year. Most professionals work within normal day hours, including realtors and bankers. It's a right to take two to three weeks of vacation at a time, two or three times a year, in concert with the school calendars. Families frequently eat at home and largely enjoy weekends outdoors/in leisure. If it's possible—let alone normal—to burn out there, how am I supposed to think about Americans who work on their vacations—if they take them at all? In the U.S., most people I knew had generally been accessible 24/7 and responsive to emails and calls any hour of the day. So many American workers live with fear of the next layoff or restructuring, given the costs of healthcare and difficulty finding another job close to home. What in the heck is this burnout thing, and is it being nurtured by normalizing the idea? Who wouldn't catch a little burnout when it comes with paid time off, professional support, and a slow return to work?

I was assured this is, indeed, a thing. It's quite serious and important, and the rewards are great for organizations that support the health and vitality of their most vulnerable members. Stress and distress go together, and modern life brings positive and negative stress in droves. At any moment, you have no idea what is happening in a colleague's whole life. Even when work is exciting, running smoothly, or organized in every way, there can be parents requiring care, sick children, household repairs requiring a lot of money, difficult relationships, heavy burdens, or personal problems taking a toll on the body, mind, and spirit. It took a little time for me to get angry about the lack of care and concern I'd witnessed for American workers and our families and to see the price I had paid for the time and energy I had stolen from my family to sneak in that one call or that little hour of emails before our day began.

In Alwin's case, we held a psychologically safe space for him to share his situation. He did take a leave of absence and embraced therapy. When he was comfortable rejoining the team, we started slowly, and colleagues tuned into his experience, sensing when he was comfortable and at ease, and when he needed a break, a walk, or space to breathe. Over time, Alwin came back to work full-time and accepted new responsibilities. Frequently, he left the lab to collaborate with his cross-functional team or meet with customers evaluating our technologies. After several years working together, Alwin was influencing commercial negotiations, sharing his knowledge and ideas to expand our reach and attract new partners. And with his experience living through burnout and emerging stronger, Alwin had a sixth sense for others with well-being at risk, the first person to put his hand on their back.

Trust and loyalty go hand in hand. When we stand by and stand with people at their most vulnerable moments, they generally pay this comfort and confidence forward. Knowing it was safe to use his voice in the most uncomfortable times, Alwin showed me when the entire team was uncomfortable with things we were testing, trying, or driving. He was a passionate creator, and I will be forever grateful for what he taught me about bright science and loving each other through the best and worst times.

IDEAS TO ACTIVATE ENGAGEMENT THROUGH LOVE AT WORK:

1. Invite all people who touch or support businesses, initiatives, or must-win efforts to explore, understand, and affect the path to the desired outcome. When you are invited to connect and collaborate but are unclear why you're there, simply ask how you can be helpful or prepare for full engagement.
2. When kicking off a team, project, venture, or new cycle, form an organizing committee to shape the session or workshop. Create an agenda that facilitates and fosters clear objectives while allowing for input and improvement. Include social time for people to connect and bond and activities that are active and fun.
3. Ask for feedback on what worked and didn't work, and give feedback if you're asked for input. This is the only way to ensure the next organizing team has the insight and information needed to improve experiences and impact.
4. Welcome outside experts, partners, or influencers to speak or collaborate on relevant topics. With our focus on the circular economy and early-stage innovation, learning from other entrepreneurs and creators was always interesting.
5. Talk about well-being and keeping a pulse on workload, stress, and whole-life health. We enjoyed physical activities and breath work

in some of our workshop agendas, accepting that some people don't like to design bridges and others hate to dance. It's all worth trying at least once.

6. When times are tight, get creative. At times when budgets were nonexistent, and travel was banned, we cared enough about our workshops and together time that we paid for it ourselves. Colleagues carpooled, lunches became potlucks, local residents offered extra bedrooms, and I personally paid for hotel rooms when people were willing to double up. Great experiences that protect alignment, resolve conflicts, and close gaps are amazing investments when turnover is nonexistent, deadlines are met, and milestones are delivered again and again.

9

ENROLLMENT

"I'm sorry, but we don't use the 'D' word around here."

—ME

To fully empower an individual, team, or organization, it's critical to understand, activate, and respect free will. Many cultures around the world domesticate humans into classes, castes, gender roles, and power paradigms. People believe their power is predetermined as a product of lineage, education, seniority, or privilege. Our learned behaviors and subconscious programs auto-populate our place in line, enable fellowship, and guide the completion of homework, projects, chores, and assignments.

The good news is that we are all perfectly capable of following directions, receiving assignments, and finishing them on time.

The bad news: Effort and energy are sub-optimized when we do not agree to do the work of our own choice and in our own way.

Over time, deeply hierarchical systems pull responsibility for strategies, priorities, and results up to executives and managers, separating themselves from the workers they are charged to activate and control. In this power paradigm, I've watched executives moving other adults between jobs and assignments like pawns on a chessboard. We can all observe the way workers are disposed of in hard times. I've also known high performers seeking a new role, only to be told, 'No. You cannot consider another position because you are extremely valuable where you are now.' In other words, a leader didn't like how much harder their work would be without a person they relied on, so they restricted the person from living their own life as they so desired. Believe me, it's inconvenient when a top performer is ready for a change. But no one is our property, our responsibility, or our slave. We get to treat and respect every human being as we would like to be treated and respected ourselves.

A complementary dynamic is an inherent human desire to serve, which is essentially loving another through an act of service. It simply feels good to be helpful and to create value with and for someone else. As we do good, we receive good in return. I have observed many examples of the return on doing a good act being many times greater than the effort shared.

When we take the time to ask someone for help and offer opportunities to take responsibility for projects, tasks, and troubleshooting, they usually say yes! And if they do say no, it's only an opportunity to understand why. Are they overloaded? Afraid? Unclear on the path forward? In conflict with others? Some pauses can be overcome, and sometimes, we must move to plan B.

INCLUSIVE HIRING PRACTICES AT NIAGA

One way to turbocharge empowerment is to hold teams accountable for hiring their new teammates. As Niaga colleagues embraced our Inclusive Interview Program, they accepted responsibility for picking the absolute best person they wanted to work with—the candidate with the right skills and experience who was ready to complement and enhance our fast-paced and milestone-driven culture.

As Niaga staffed up to support growth, eight to ten peers were involved in every hiring decision. This process took about six weeks after candidates were identified, and we were lucky to have fifty-plus applicants for open roles (a testament to the human desire for meaningful, purpose-full work).

HERE'S HOW THE SIX-WEEK PROCESS UNFOLDS:

Round 1: Identify 16 diverse candidates, with a minimum of 8 female candidates. The first 16 candidates were selected by a corporate recruiter and me from as many as 95 initial applicants. These 16 candidates completed an online interview using an application called HireVue. Through video and written responses to 6-8 questions, all candidates were asked the same questions in the same way. Four people reviewed the responses and paired the candidate slate down to 8. All 8 candidate profiles were shared with the entire Niaga interview team.

Round 2: Live interviews for 8 candidates, seeking 4 candidates for Round 3. Three pairs of Niaga interviewers screened all 8 candidates with specific competencies in mind. Scheduling candidates and interviewers with full-time responsibilities was tricky, but we completed these 24 interviews in a week. After all 24 conversations were complete, the entire Niaga interview team listened to the feedback, and 8 candidates became 4.

Round 3: Live interviews for 4 candidates by 2 new pairs of interviewers, seeking two candidates for Round 4. These interviewers had participated in each round of feedback, and their mission was to explore and test specific insights or concerns identified in Round 2. After these 8 meetings were complete, all Niaga interviewers met for feedback, and 4 candidates were whittled down to the final 2.

Round 4: Case Study Presentations for the final 2 candidates. The last 2 candidates were asked to complete and present a case study appropriate for the function and team. All Niaga interviewers listened to the presentations and met one last time to select the candidate for a formal offer.

The decision on the final candidate was made by the specific team adding the role, following our consent decision-making process. It was not most important to have consensus or complete agreement—the hiring team was empowered to choose the candidate they believed in most and felt most comfortable working with, as milestone delivery and performance were their responsibility in the end.

Inevitably, many top candidates were managers and directors in the past, and in expressing their strengths, it was common to hear that they were very good at DELEGATION.

"Ut oh... I'm sorry, but you're not going to be able to use that word around here," was always my response. You see, in a culture with zero subordination and maximum appreciation we're each one adult with twenty-four hours in a day. We don't have big people and little people. If you'd like someone to build something, fix something, change something, or deliver something, you need to enroll them in the unmet need and ask for their help with it. Our team is small, and expertise generally falls into a specific person's camp, but that doesn't mean they have to do anything. They get to help, and when the need is clear, the work is important, and the priorities for the team are aligned, you can count on the people around here to do the right thing with passion and conviction.

We were fortunate to attract several excellent teammates who were great contributors to our progress and performance. Nico Janssen, who was hired through a 100% online process during COVID work-from-home times, shared how his entire family was engaged in the round-by-round experience, similar to watching *The Voice of Holland* on TV. My favorite observations of the process were a deep awareness of the work ahead and the culture when candidates and teammates had great exposure to each other before Day One. The personal responsibility teams showed for the new colleagues' success got them through the highs and lows when they had made the hiring decision. This is quite different from a typical hiring decision made by a manager, with a new employee 'surprise!' for the working team.

Adopting this protocol may take more time and energy, but I promise the return on inclusivity and empowerment will be worth it.

LOVING LEADERSHIP ACTIONS TO HONOR FREE WILL:

1. Hire people with demonstrated capacity to think for themselves while contributing to strong teams. It is a great superpower to organize and activate others, and all strong teams have individuals who enjoy that contribution to structure and cohesiveness. Unleashing the diversity of the best teams comes with honoring each person's unique needs, motivations, and creative juices, respecting that there are extroverts and introverts, early birds and night owls, grinders and pacers, and hunters and farmers. When we take the time to identify the goals, plan the work, and work the plan together, each person enrolled in their contribution and agreeing to the delivery dates and deadlines will play their part in concert.

2. Develop coaches, not teachers: Teachers tell, while coaches question. There's a time for teaching and training; providing instruction, direction, and skill development is critical in any enterprise. In daily life with competent and experienced adults, though, teammates and leaders who collaborate on possible solutions and help each other think for themselves will activate a lot more energy, engagement, and creation. Basic coaching questions like, "How would you approach this situation?" Or "Can we think of three different ways to get from here to there?" Or "What do you think Barack Obama and Donald Trump would do right now?", "What else have we considered?", and "Does anyone else see this differently?"

3. Embrace the idea that 'Nos Are Free' in all conversations and allow people to ask any question without retribution. When we accept that the worst thing we could ever hear in most scenarios is "No," it's amazing how many times the actual answer is "Yes," "Maybe," or "Tell me more." This applies to negotiations, enrolling people in change, requesting compensation reviews, applying for new responsibilities, or asking for help. Play with asking for the absurd just to expand the capacity to ask for help and enroll others.

4. Turn roadblocks into dialogue by exploring 'why.' It's very tempting to make assumptions about why others behave or react in a certain way, but the only way to know for sure is to ask. Admittedly, I was a terrible ass-umer in the past. I had very low emotional intelligence and zero empathy as a financial analyst and finance manager in my early years. My love of numbers, logic, spreadsheets, and data-based storytelling left me beloved by fellow number crunchers, introverts, and similar smarty-pant types. Little did I know, though, that my peers and leaders in sales and marketing

roles were not the biggest fans. I was completely unaware of this gap, happy with my cool, calm, and consistent lens on the world. I didn't even notice they didn't particularly like me because I didn't sense or feel their distance. I also didn't care to measure it. It took being passed over for a promotion to learn WHY I hadn't won the role, and the zero-empathy problem finally required some attention. In parallel, my very emotive husband was completely unhappy with my righteousness, expressing his discontent and pain while I explained precisely why his feelings were invalid in each fight. I'm forever grateful to the coaches and counselors who helped me understand empathy. Developing the capacity to think with my mind AND feel with my heart was life-changing, as if the world went from black and white to technicolor.

Let me save you thousands of dollars in therapy, coaches, marriage counselors, and divorce settlements with these simple exercises to experience the magic of activating loving curiosity and care-full connection:

1. Spend an entire day only asking questions of people around you. With genuine curiosity and an open heart, park where you are, what you believe, and what you know to meet people where they are today. These skills can be refreshed with a stranger on an airplane, a colleague you see every day, your partner at home, or a child at college.

2. Whenever you hear something that makes you uncomfortable in any way, recognize the physical sensations and pause. Instead of reacting, defending, or challenging, simply say, "Hmmm... tell me more..." I have enjoyed the dialogue that follows this simple prompt so much that I tattooed it on my left arm as a reminder.

This simple pause has allowed me to suspend my instinct and intuition—which I used to trust blindly—to hear new insights and information as another person sees the situation or opportunity in an entirely new way. I already know what I know and believe about absolutely everything, but I do not know what you know, where you are, what you believe, or what you prefer until you tell me. And once I can understand where I am, where you are, and the space in between, we can identify the best way to get wherever we want to go together.

3. Try to assume people have good intentions and that we're all wired to meet our own needs before serving others. Intent and impact are not always aligned, but if we can generally believe people are doing their best and full of desire to do the right thing, we can hold the space for conversation when intent was good, but impact was bad.

   For example, a former colleague was chronically late, which used to irk me. As a punctual person who strives to be someone people can rely on, I took the disrespect for my time and others' time personally.

   My stories and attachment to punctuality left me in judgment about his behaviors, even when I adored him and treasured working on projects together. After reconsidering his behaviors, preferences, and work style from a place of compassion and curiosity, I found space to let him be himself while staying true to my values *for me*.

   We discussed our approaches to managing time and came to an agreement: When I was responsible for an agenda or meeting facilitation, I would be early and start on time. If he was overscheduled or delayed, he could skip the meeting or join late. When he was the organizer or lead for a meeting, we could arrive and start as he wished. This was a win-win that allowed each of us to be ourselves while meeting our independent needs as a team.

10

THE TRUTH ABOUT TRUST

"Razor blades and I have never been friends, and I have the scars to prove it."

—ME

Integrity and trust are two virtues most humans treasure, although our ideals often conflict with the behaviors and actions we observe and the (frequently harder to see) behaviors and actions we take ourselves. We repeat thoughts on trust like, "Trust but verify," "Trust is earned," or "You can never trust those people."

A story I've told throughout my life goes like this: Losing trust is like a house burning down. You can rebuild a house after a fire, but it takes eighteen months and is never quite the same. The consequences for losing trust were devastating and long-lasting, and this story reinforced the commonly held belief that *people can forgive, but they never forget.*

With this frame of trust, I aspired to top behavior while feeling pressured to be perfectly consistent. I deeply feared falling or failing. I wanted to be trusted, to be seen by others as trustworthy, and to deserve a reputation for being someone you can count on to a) be on time, b) do the right thing, and c) deliver on my promises. Don't we all want to be seen in the best light and to live with integrity with our word?

On the positive side, I was generally a high performer and on time for meetings and appointments AT WORK. Sadly, my kid's day care probably made more money off my late pickup fees (which were $50 per five minutes) than the tuition. On the negative side, though, I became very judgmental toward people who struggled with time management or completing tasks on time, and I would lay in bed after most important meetings replaying what everyone had said and done and how I had performed, scrubbing my words and behaviors for things I could have or should have done differently.

As an employee at Avery Dennison, their greatest gift to me was consistent access to training programs and coaches. Around 2013, I had the good fortune to work with a coach from Franklin Covey named Andy Cindrich, who taught me how to apply the principles from *The Speed of Trust* and *4 Disciplines of Execution* in my role as VP of Sales for Materials Group North America. In *The Speed of Trust*, Stephen Covey Jr. cites trust as the #1 leadership competency of the 21st century, and I have come to agree with him.

Since this book is excellent and readily available to all, I will not repeat the principles. In my own experience and observation, the single greatest skill to sustain high trust has more to do with addressing problems than being perfect at every turn.

Building and protecting trust relies on REPAIRING and RESTORING trust that falls. As I've loosened my grip on perfection and grabbed responsibility for owning mistakes and doing the right thing, I've experienced the transformation that comes from living through something difficult together. When done well, relationships are better and deeper after a problem or disagreement than if the problem never happened in the first place.

Every company selling a product or service has an unhappy or unsatisfied customer from time to time. Very angry customers at my company skipped the line and went directly to the CEO of the entire corporation, seeking urgent action and support. There's nothing like a red-hot threat of lost business and lawsuits to kick-start a lively day at the office!

In my experience, this energy doesn't sit at the corporate headquarters for long. Within the hour, five of us were dropping everything to learn everything we could about a customer receiving a roll of our materials in Colorado. Printers worldwide purchased very large rolls of pressure-sensitive label stock from us and ran them through presses where images were printed and shapes cut to create the stickers for jars, boxes, wine bottles, and the like.

On this day, while the label material roll was on press and unwinding into the printer, a razor blade flew out of the roll, which could have seriously injured the press operator. Our company had a reputation for high quality and safe operations, but this could have been a serious situation, and the company owner was extremely angry—ready to move his business and insisting on a response.

Our team was shocked and concerned, even in disbelief this could have happened in our manufacturing and distribution operations. We organized our approach to investigating the claim and called the gentleman to acknowledge the pain, apologize, and share that we were starting an investigation. We promised to be back within a week to share insights and communicate the corrective actions.

Over the week, we learned a slitter operator in an Avery Dennison distribution center had made a small but very impactful choice. A slitter is a big machine that takes a huge, heavy roll of label materials on one side and runs it through a series of rotating knives to "slit" the big roll into several smaller rolls with specific widths for a label converter's narrow printing press. As an example, a two-meter-wide master roll might become ten smaller rolls six inches to thirty inches wide.

This operator was experiencing adhesive buildup on the rotating knives that cut the large roll into segments. When the machine was stopped between roll changes, he would use a razor blade to scrape the excess adhesive residue off the knives, always wearing protective gear as required. When the work was done, though, he had set the blade on top of the machine frame, which vibrates while operating. This razor blade had fallen into the roll and been wrapped up in the material.

Corrective actions were taken, standard work was modified, tools were changed, and the operator completed additional training on blade safety and preventative maintenance of his equipment. In addition, our safety and claims teammates provided an honest report to the customer's team, sharing the investigation, the outcome, and the actions taken to ensure this could never happen again. The customer was so satisfied with the outcome that they asked our people to visit and train their team on how to handle complaints and claims.

I've now experienced the power of intentional REACTION to conflicts, claims, concerns, and crises. It is normal to feel defensive, scared, fearful, or panicked when things go wrong in relationships, transactions, or events. Our bodies are always ready for fight or flight, and when all that adrenaline gets released into the system, it's good to run if a bear is over your shoulder, but it's best to pause and breathe if death is not imminent.

Not every problem is as obvious as a razor blade in a roll of sticker paper, but most things that challenge our sense of security, raise potential risk, or incite pain are triggered by differences in our beliefs, styles, behaviors, and perceptions. Teams have very diverse ways of addressing conflict, expressing differences, exploring options, and settling scores. Reward systems often pit one department against another, reinforcing desired outcomes or targets while limiting the capacity to simply do the right thing.

A STORY OF DIVIDENDS FROM EXTENDING TRUST...

It's important to extend trust and embrace learning by doing to maximize empowerment. Activating the experience, curiosity, and creativity of diverse teams requires a comfort level with variability and quick course correction when situations are sub-optimal. For each mistake to learn from, an equally interesting breakthrough or solution is likely emerging from expertise in action. Kaizen is an excellent tool for pulling small groups into continuous improvement, and it can be equally applied to factory floors, sales pipelines, and office workflows.

Kaizen is a Japanese term for constant small change for the better. It is a highly inclusive and empowering approach, giving teams responsibility and tools to identify and implement positive change, which can involve simplifying processes, reconsidering policies, or organizing things in new ways.

The customer service team at Avery Dennison's materials group was well-managed and highly regarded by customers and sales teams. They leveraged an "Effortless Experience" approach driven by their director, Anita Sturtz, where any activity that stopped their ability to handle a customer's needs on the first call was documented and addressed. Over time, most situations could be managed quickly, but one area that was difficult for customers and the service team involved expedited freight. At times when the customers' needs were intense and solutions were urgent and important, our best practices in procurement and expense management required three carrier quotations. In their defense, the transportation team was very strong and responsive. We also faced inconsistent policies around who pays for expedites, which can leave the freight costing almost as much as the product in extreme cases.

In its current state at the time, customer service had zero power or authority to make decisions on expedited freight, and sales management and transportation colleagues both had to approve expedited decisions given their financial consequences. It's highly likely that department and individual goals tied to annual budgets and bonuses reinforced a desire for fewer expedites and lower transportation costs quarter by quarter and year over year.

As we were focused on trust, empowerment, and customer satisfaction, we decided to test the most empowered version of this activity. In the first call, we received support to carve out a $250,000 budget for our customer service team to expedite decisions on the spot. With many of them on these phones for more than twenty years, they knew how these situations played out, how expedites worked, and how much they cost. They also knew which customers found themselves in a pinch most frequently, as well as how to reach their colleagues in transportation to arrange whatever was required at a good cost. And they knew how to negotiate a win-win outcome on a case-by-case basis.

As we relieved sales managers from their role in the decision process (because they were hard to track down given sales activities on the road and meetings with clients, delaying approvals) and changed the quote requirements, we improved the speed of response. We modified systems to allow customer service to add expedite fees or surcharges to invoices. We asked them to share their stories about how they each handled difficult situations so they could learn from each other and best practices could be standardized.

We may not have had the absolute possible lowest cost in the end, but after six months of putting decision-making responsibilities in the front line's hands, observing their decisions, and creating space for too much or not enough from time to time, the total cost of their expedited freight decisions was a fraction of the former expense, and only $70,000 had been spent with much more invoiced to the customers willing to solve their own problems at their own expense.

LOVING LEADERSHIP ACTIONS TO TREASURE TRUST:

1. Identify sources of customer dissatisfaction and try to quantify the cost of fallen trust in your company. If you look back at five years of sales data, most firms have lost a paying customer. When long-term customers change their purchasing behavior, it's important to ask why. Through analysis, I found several instances where customer quality claims were denied or 'non-verified' after an internal evaluation. While the company may have avoided an immediate $30,000 or $40,000 expense to replace materials or refund an order, on more than one occasion, customers moved business to competitors to the tune of $750,000 to $3,000,000. The claim and lost sales don't appear related in short-term reporting, but the relationship between dissatisfaction and consequence is easy to see over a longer period of time. I'm happy to share that a sincere apology and effort to correct mistakes made years in the past restored purchasing and growth from these clients. I'm proud to share that some of these customers have called years later with job offers—a clear sign that restoring and repairing trust pays dividends again and again.

2. For any company, activating the team's capacity to act quickly, do the right thing, and adapt as they go requires training on trust dynamics. Encourage dialogue about trust falls and role-play crucial conversations. Give teams support to put the love of the customer and delightful customer experiences at the center of everything. It's way more important to be trusted to do the right thing time and time again than to be right, to never make mistakes, or to hold every existing policy or procedure as gospel. When customers feel seen, understood, supported, and proud to work with our services, products, and people, they will keep giving us their hard-earned money to do what we do. Treasure them. Treasure each other and create positive outcomes wherever you get the chance to serve or improve.

3. Ask about trust by adding retrospective pauses to agendas with teams, strategic customers, or primary suppliers. In addition to the business priorities and initiatives, ask how things are going in the relationship with the key players and the firms overall. Good questions are specific and open: On a scale of 1-10, how would you rate the level of trust in our relationship as partners? What would it take to get a higher rating? If you compare us to your highest trust relationships, where are others serving you better? Do you feel like we understand your business and truly listen to your needs for today and tomorrow?

4. If you complete a customer or employee engagement or satisfaction survey, add a few questions about trust within teams, between teams, and overall. Take the results back to the participants with insights and open questions to explore gaps and possibilities. Vulnerability is an asset; as said before, we can't fix what we can't see.

While 70–75% satisfaction may be the top quartile for satisfaction in many industries, I don't understand why 1/4 people unsatisfied or dissatisfied are acceptable to any high-performance enterprise.

11

FIERCE INCLUSION

"Tell me please... Would you one time just let me be myself?"

—3 DOORS DOWN

Eight months into the 'drama-free' partnership at Niaga, teammates expressed interest in a new organizational structure to bring our circular economy ambitions to life. We were already in small groups on key initiatives, so leaning into agile work and empowerment felt worth exploring.

We formed a team to study alternatives and shape new possibilities, reserving rights for everyone else to be an editor or challenger. The design team educated themselves with books, TED Talks and documentaries like *Holocracy*, *Sociocracy 3.0*, *Aequacy* and other 'future of work' models. We learned from the experiences of Ricardo Semler, Ray Dalio, Giovanna D'Alessio, and more while holding space to customize the best approach for Niaga. Over the course of three design workshops, a new structure emerged: A team-based, high-empowerment system respecting best practices like the Bell Mason venturing framework and complementing compliance programs at our corporate parent, DSM.

The design team considered research cited in *Aequacy* from one thousand US and European companies. This data reported the most frequent adjectives used by employees to describe culture at the most hierarchical firms and the adjectives used at the most empowered firms. These insights led to twelve core values, framing elements of culture worth protecting. Two became game-changers at Niaga: Fierce Inclusion and Radical Transparency.

Diversity and inclusion have been hot topics for decades now, and 2022 research by Harvard Business School faculty member Amy Edmondson showed homogenous teams outperform diverse teams quite consistently... until she took a closer look at the outliers. The most diverse teams delivered the best results in a small cluster, and instead of throwing out the small cluster of data points, she reached out to understand WHY these positive deviants were shining. The primary driver of diverse team performance was psychological safety, discussed in Chapter 2. With a focus on diversity without investment in equity and deep inclusion, leveraging our collective power remains elusive in many organizations.

In my opinion, it's easy enough to improve diversity. If you set metrics clearly enough, high-performing teams will hit them. When targets for more women, more races, more LGTBQ+ representation, more [xyz] are reached, I've seen male leaders declare success and celebrate 'mission accomplished.' I owe some portion of my own rise into executive roles to the gender diversity targets set by Avery Dennison's top management. In one year, 22% of director and VP positions were to be filled by ladies. Low-and-behold, several penis-less persons were more than happy to rise to the occasion.

Unfortunately, mixing things up does not create or guarantee inclusion all by itself. One year after DSM delivered on a massive shift in female leadership, 95% of the executive men responded positively to an engagement survey question about feeling supported and valued at work. Only 52% of the executive female respondents felt the same way. Diversity? A+. Inclusion? C minus (C-) at best.

In my first months of management team meetings after being promoted to the VP/GM level, I regularly listened and observed with little space to contribute. When I spoke up from a different point of view, it was as if I gave words, but others received radio static. When a male colleague repeated exactly what I said, the thought was met with "Great idea!" or "Brilliant thought, Brian!" while my temperature rose inside. Over time, I developed terrible habits: talking louder, cutting people off, challenging people who didn't let me finish, and speaking up for women who weren't comfortable taking space themselves. Like Nancy Pelosi and Rush Limbaugh, any antics of animated men were tolerated if not encouraged, while the women with opinions were forceful, bitchy, or behaving badly.

Access to women's networks, training opportunities, and mentors helped me navigate the Narrow Band over the years. The Narrow Band represents the specific set of acceptable behaviors and styles for female leaders where we're not too much like men—no cursing, visible anger, aggression, managed assertion. And not too much like a woman—no tears, limited attention to soft topics, asexuality, and seriousness without being rigid.

With constant attention and awareness navigating this narrow band, what started out feeling like a tightrope one thousand feet off the ground without a safety net eased into a feeling like a wide balance beam a few inches off the floor. With more confidence and invitations to contribute from male peers, I earned a comfortable seat at the table. Male peers became collaborators and friends. We invested in peer feedback, culture, and climate studies, and time to understand our differences and leverage our strengths. Yet, even with all this effort, many top ladies left the firm one by one—including me.

At Niaga, we had a chance to create a culture from scratch and bring it to life. We could be a part of something new and different, where a diverse team could fight for the right to be themselves and navigate the inevitable conflicts that come with diversity. We could have chosen 'inclusion' as a core value, but we chose FIERCE inclusion. What did that mean?

In a fiercely inclusive organization, we each stand as one person twenty-four hours a day, giving our time and energy to contribute to a mission and journey for which we're ultimately equally responsible. Each teammate is a talented, experienced adult who accepts personal responsibility to deliver on our commitments. When we bring our authentic selves to the table and stretch beyond our comfort zones, positive and negative stresses will create pressure.

When the pressure rises, subconscious programming eventually hijacks our senses and sensibilities. On any given day, a person of any race, gender, age, or experience can be at odds with the person sitting next to them. In a fiercely inclusive environment, we get to be different, we get to be emotional, we get to argue our points, we get to share, and we must listen—with the comfort and confidence that no matter how heated or crazy it gets, we are supported in revisiting, releasing, replacing, repairing, and restoring trust.

We built tools to support collective contribution to ideas and problem solving so all minds were engaged and voices were heard. In Niaga workshops, we placed comment cards with thought starters at every chair in our sessions. These cards offered an opportunity to contribute something tangible and enduring to the topic at hand. More importantly, the cards activated deeper listening by extroverts when responses came in text over voice, and the cards offered introverts a place to share input and ideas without having to compete for air time. I struggled to hold my own tongue and thanked coaches for nudges like 'Kelly, there's a reason we're designed with one mouth and two ears.'

The most diverse teams occasionally found themselves in crisis, frustrated by their disagreements or difficulty making decisions. A coach for each team played a very important role early on, supporting individuals and the collective in deep understanding, teaching consent versus consensus, and asking us to pause to reflect on ourselves and each other along the way.

One afternoon, we paused to mark the retirement of Huub Omloo, a regulatory affairs expert who joined Niaga at the end of a forty-year career with DSM. Huub brought his love to work every day, leveraging technical understanding, deep experience writing and negotiating global standards, and uncanny creativity in strategic positioning and political awareness. He was a quirky guy with an effervescent personality and generous spirit. On the day of his retirement, we were trying to celebrate Huub, but he's the one who came with the best gifts.

Huub gave me a tart pan with a recipe and ingredients for a local Limburg dish called lentil pie, written in the form of an ISO standard. It touched my heart, but not as much as the words he held for Valerie Reid, our innovation director. Huub shared his experience at Niaga as a highlight in his entire career, describing the culture as follows: "I've worked in many teams in my life and experienced a lot of competition, a lot of criticism, and a lot of encouragement. On the best days, I knew the people around me would give me a hand. But here, I feel like you have your hand on my back... as if you're always there to support my ideas and needs no matter what."

This was the day I knew we were doing something different that felt so right... If a part-time working, Disney-loving, Harley-riding, committee-chairing, standard-setting retiree wanted to keep working with us and felt our hands on his back every single day, the culture was evolving just fine.

ACTIONS TO ACTIVATE FIERCE INCLUSION THROUGH LOVING LEADERSHIP:

1. How much diversity can you truly see, and how much personality and style does your culture tolerate? I watched an entirely white, male leadership team pat themselves on the back for having 'thought diversity' because they celebrated their mix of introverts, extroverts, thinkers, feelers, and ages across the thirties, forties, and fifties representing three to four different states/countries. Of course, all the women and minorities who heard this proclamation wished it was a joke, and some of us proactively acknowledged and apologized for their unconscious bias. It is one thing to see our colors, gender expressions, personalities, styles, and behaviors. It is next-level to see, understand, test, and tolerate the differences. On another level, we explore, express, evaluate, accept, and activate our styles and preferences. In the best of all worlds, we get to enjoy, accentuate, empower, celebrate, and leverage the counterforces in complementary strengths and weaknesses. It takes courage to ask for feedback on the dynamics in teams at any level, and small steps like 1-on-1 conversations might be a safer place to start the journey than big team reflection sessions. Plenty of coaches and consultants can facilitate surveys and assessments like the Discovery Insights profile or Culture and Climate Surveys.

I'll share a personal example, crediting Darrell Hughes and Scott Hornsby for our leadership team's work to see our collective strengths and release tension in Avery Dennison's Materials Group.

For quite some time, as VP of Sales in our division, I had not particularly enjoyed working with Jason, our VP of Finance. It felt like each time I had a big idea for an initiative or project to drive positive change, he was a wet blanket on my fire with twenty-five skeptical questions and every reason something might not work. During a leadership workshop, surveys about our styles and preferences led to individual scores on a scale of pragmatism and proof versus vision and intuition. When we took our places standing on a line on the floor stretching from -40 (most pragmatic) to +40 (most intuitive) based on our scores, I was not the highest on vision and intuition, but I recognized my company on this scale. I can admit I was quite comfortable being in this cluster, firmly entrenched in my biases.

I looked far to my right to see Jason down the line with those who managed risk and measured everything twice. Only after embracing his strengths and my own did I accept that Jason's challenges and questions improved the probability of success by proactively exploring risks and tending to details. After Jason heard my frustrations, feeling like he never supported my dreams, he realized taking a moment to show support and enthusiasm for concepts before chopping them into bite-sized pieces would put me at ease. In no time at all, we enjoyed our work together, and a lifetime friendship flowed as tension dissolved naturally. I'm a big fan of Jason to this day!

2. Create space for options and alternatives: One of the best things about the most diverse teams is the breadth of approaches different people take to creating and problem-solving. By engaging

groups in questions and using drawings and single words on paper to pull everyone into the dialogue, we get to see and hear many alternative perspectives, but we also get to learn how individuals communicate, how they think, how they behave, and how they react. Push the boundaries of exploration by asking for the absurd and extreme edges of possibility, and practice 'for-ness.' When the boundaries of current thinking are rigid, asking everyone in a diverse group what WOULD make the most unbelievable ideas possible can make novel solutions appear. Improving competence in broadening possibilities before selecting the best path to the outcome is not only helpful, but it can also protect an element of playfulness and fun.

3. Get creative in soliciting feedback and insight from others, activating pulse surveys, holding roundtable lunches, administering 360-degree feedback,[1] and monitoring employee and customer satisfaction. When gaps exist, ask the survey participants for their unmet needs and actions to improve the climate or culture for them and for all. Resist the temptation to assume leaders have all the answers and the best ideas are held at the top. We can't fix what we can't see, and openness to receive insight into gaps gives holes and valleys shape and texture. We can fill the gaps quite quickly when customers and teammates bring passion, energy, and love to safe spaces and put the best ideas to work.

---

[1] 360-degree feedback gathers input from a variety of sources, traditionally supervisors, peers, and subordinates. I've encouraged teammates to request input from internal and external contacts, frequently including customers and suppliers. With more inputs, the recipient of feedback has diverse reflections of strengths and opportunities for further growth. Feedback is presented anonymously, and any coach should be prepared for recipients to focus on the negative feedback when it's equally important, if not more important, to recognize and validate strengths.

4. Cross the chasm between office doors and factory floors with mandatory hands-on experiences for new employees at all levels. After my MBA internship at Frontier Cooperative Herbs, I was hired into a full-time role as marketing manager for Frontier's organic coffee business. While most of my responsibilities were performed from a cubicle in an open-air office in Cedar Rapids, Iowa, I was required to work at the coffee roasting plant every Wednesday of my first year. At first, it was fun to make the drive to Urbana to see the roasters, experience the packaging lines, and work side-by-side with the team in the factory.

   After months, though, I felt like I'd learned everything, and it started feeling like a waste of time—until the day of the fire. One of the roasters caught fire while a batch was in process. If I hadn't been at the factory that day, I wouldn't have experienced the safety response, the calm and collected emergency procedures, and the way the well-managed and deeply supported team stuck together when chaos knocked.

   Looking back on this orientation program, I would highly encourage any manufacturing company to require hands-on experiences for white-collar workers. The relationships built across the organization are just as useful as the deep knowledge of the product, costs, productivity, and customer awareness in every corner of the firm.

12

RADICAL TRANSPARENCY

"Sunlight is the best disinfectant."

—U.S. SUPREME COURT JUSTICE LOUIS BRANDIES

Leaning into the with you, not to you promise, Niaga pushed the envelope on radical transparency within the team and in the world. As stewards and champions of a circular economy, we believe everyone deserves to know what is in stuff and that participation in all things should be activated with free will.

RADICAL TRANSPARENCY – EXTERNAL PERSPECTIVES

If you have the luxury of creating something with all available knowledge and the space to redesign products and systems for health and vitality in the long-term, materials used in things should be safe and non-toxic, and things should be put together in ways that allow taking apart and repurposing all materials down the road. To this end, when we were creating new materials and new methods for recyclable carpets, mattresses, and furniture, we wanted to provide all stakeholders with the ingredients used in stuff, just as food labels around the world are regulated to explain ingredients and nutritional facts. We strove to regulate digital passports for all things in the world. Requiring return instructions could keep goods out of landfills and incinerators, establishing endless loops of refurbished, recycled, and reused components, free of toxic ingredients and single-use status.

Niaga regarded our external stakeholders as partners through our ventures' Concept, Seed, and Alpha phases. Instead of typical strategic or transactional relationships with suppliers and customers, we intentionally sought greater intimacy and alignment, knowing we had to prove technical feasibility, customize solutions, troubleshoot with urgency, and complete closed loops behind products bearing our brand. Partners were not targeted on size or financial capacities alone; we assessed the fit with the venture phase based on attitudes toward sustainability, existing portfolio innovations, leadership in the industry, and alignment with our mission and goals.

Object Carpet in Germany is a great example of this partnership in action. As a family-owned business, Object has always held a nice balance between today's leadership and results, selling top-quality, high-design carpets and protecting its legacy as a steward of recycling, waste reduction, renewable energy, and sustainability. While Niaga's innovators, engineers, chemists, and anthropologists brought science, materials, equipment, pilot production lines, and big ideas to the table, the Object Team brought decades of carpet design, deep knowledge of fibers, manufacturing experience, and market access to the collaboration. Transparency was tested, and ownership of ideas and outcomes were debated, but overall, the results speak for themselves: Object Carpet was the first manufacturer in Europe to fully integrate the Niaga production system into their factory. They built a beautiful "glass manufacture" showroom in Krefeld,

Germany to openly share the technology and teach the value chain about circular economies, design for reuse, and carpet recycling. Our leadership in changing a massive industry was recognized with many awards, and you can learn more at Object Carpet's website anytime.

The first adopters of a new technology took a leap of faith together, facing uncertainty, challenges, and inevitable setbacks. Navigating bad days and bad news requires courage and trust. We learned transparency and vulnerability pay off every single time.

RADICAL TRANSPARENCY – INSIDE THE ORGANIZATION

Hierarchical organizations often leave the big decisions and direction setting to small teams in small rooms, debating and choosing the paths and policies and unveiling or cascading them through the organization. It's basically accepted that the people with the best titles and highest compensation know the most and are positioned to make the best decisions on behalf of everyone else. When the decisions are high stakes, like choosing whose jobs to eliminate in a restructuring or merging with another firm, lawyers join the party with secrecy agreements, retention bonuses, and terrible consequences if the trust is violated. When I signed these agreements, I never told a soul, including my spouse.

Niaga colleagues activated radical transparency in many ways. All teammates participated in team workshops three times each year, and every teammate served on planning and organizing committees. Ninety-five percent of the group completed every post-event, engagement, or well-being survey, providing essential insights to shape and improve future programs. 360-degree feedback was generously completed by almost all teammates and most external contributors when asked.

The venture was governed by a source team, not a management team. The source team included the managing director, chief technology officer, controller, and one representative from each of the growth teams (carpet, mattress, panels) and support teams (manufacturing, innovation, radical transparency and movement mobilizers). When the source team held meetings to review financial performance, discuss challenges, or change policies and procedures, any Niaga colleague was welcome to listen in. When COVID-19 forced everyone to communicate through video calls, the source team representatives would meet on camera, and anyone else in the organization could dial in to listen off camera, participating in the discussion through the chat.

This level of transparency did make life difficult. In one workshop, we were facing financial challenges and needed to reduce expenses in the coming year. All the teams had presented their annual plans and critical projects, and as a team of thirty, we had to prioritize all of them and stop or pause many to protect a few.

The debate was fierce, and our commitment to consent-based decision-making over consensus ruffled some feathers. Each team took the first pass to sift and sort through their lists to elevate a select few. This phase of the work went well, but the total number of projects was still too high for our small but mighty team to complete on time and on budget. A few more projects needed to be moved to the parking lot or trash can before our planning work was complete.

When the debate had run its course, one controversial project made it through to GO status. This involved leveraging Niaga carpet technology and materials to redesign artificial turf. As you can imagine, our passionate team of game-changers and planet-savers was fractured over the mere idea of making something artificial, unnatural, and fundamentally unnecessary, sustainable or recyclable. This was one case where maybe we should let Mother Nature win and return to playing on good old green grass.

Niaga was already involved in a program with the Dutch government and two collaborating parties. Three parties won a substantial grant to test and prove the viability of a recyclable artificial turf. Our research and trials had delivered enough proof points to suggest it was feasible, but it was just not easy. On that day, I was the decision-maker who used consent to say yes after all dissent was understood. I left that workshop with a few very angry colleagues, extremely frustrated by their canceled projects while this ugly one lived on.

So, what happens in a radically transparent and fiercely inclusive world when tempers flare, and decisions don't go with the majority? We connect, listen, explore, soothe, and study. We respect the passion and energy that fuels the frustration. After all, the care, investment, and love of the mission are behind the big feelings when buttons are pushed and tempers flare. Eventually, we embraced the path again as the WHYs behind the decisions were understood, and hands returned to each other's backs.

I missed one opportunity to drive radical transparency in 2020, and I regret it to this day. As COVID-19 swept through the world and one country after another reacted to the threat, DSM locked things down in the spirit of safety and risk mitigation as fast as any corporation. With the heightened risk in the world and attention to conserving cash, we started considering all measures necessary to protect our teams and vital interests.

This timing coincided with an active initiative to rethink our global innovation and research and development resources and structures, and a headcount reduction target was part of the grand plan. COVID-19 uncertainties accelerated decision-making and implementation of these cost-reduction and expense-management programs.

I've been on the decision-making side of restructuring actions six times in my life, and I've always felt a bit disgusted by the entire thing. First, underperforming teammates deserve honest conversations about their fit with the roles and responsibilities of the job they're not delivering. When expectations are clear, and skills or motivation aren't there, most people will act on an opportunity to try something new in a different area or find a better fit in another company. Very rarely have I put someone on a performance improvement plan who ended up being fired—they either rose to the occasion with awareness of the improvements needed, moved to a different role that was a better fit for their skills or interests, or sensed the writing on the wall and applied for jobs outside of the company.

So... when this very typical implementation of a very typical restructuring process trickled down to me with a headcount target of four and the corresponding annual cost reduction target, I signed a secrecy agreement and went into the shadows with the business controller to consider the team and consequences. We developed scenarios, presented possibilities, received feedback from attorneys and human resources colleagues, and rinsed, and repeated.

In the background, with my promises of radical transparency and fierce inclusion in mind, I explored alternate outcomes to deliver the same cost-savings benefit. Taking a key from friends and colleagues at other companies, I explored asking our teammates if anyone was interested in dropping down to a 0.9 or 0.8 part-time schedule. If everyone on our team shifted to a half-day off each week or a full day off every two weeks, we could deliver 80% of the target, saving three roles. Half of the team already had flexible schedules, so it worked fine in many cases. I also explored early retirement possibilities, and none of these choices were possible for two reasons: 1) the broader corporation didn't have the policies or mechanisms in place to support it, and 2) the initiative's goals were communicated as full time equivalent (FTE) eliminations (headcount numbers), not financial savings. The FTE count was the most important thing.

As a team, we went through the process of saying goodbye to four colleagues in September of 2020. As someone who was fired once, I know no severance payment or lengthy transition plan can fill the hole in your heart when someone says your position is no longer needed and it's time to carry on without you around. Even as COVID kept people apart, social distance was respected, masks were an article of clothing, and most hotel rooms and train cars were empty, so we brought the team together. I was advised not to do this by more than one voice, but this group I loved deserved to go through the most difficult moment we'd faced as a team.

Everyone knew decision day was coming, but two of us knew who was being affected. Slowly but surely, one morning, conversations were had with the four teammates who would be leaving Niaga and DSM in the months ahead. We cried and handed each other tissues. We took walks and thanked the people facing the changes ahead. I felt terrible, and yet I did my best to provide context and support to the individuals who had given so much and the entire team in a setback and dark moment we got to experience together.

I'm pleased to report that everyone ended up in new situations, as most do, and the rest of the team felt a tremendous new responsibility to deliver on our milestones and targets. The only way we could protect each other and set up for adding talent instead of relieving it was to prove the technologies, win with partners, and build the circular models out in the world.

If I could have a do-over, I would engage the entire adult team in an adult conversation about our real situation. If we, as a team, needed to create $250,000 of value quickly, I would engage everyone in dialogue about how to activate that. I believe that if I had shared the urgent need to reduce expenses in any way possible, several things would have come to light that I didn't see on my own. If I had asked, I would have known that one teammate's husband had a role in London, and she wanted to move there with him to start a family. Her role could have been eliminated instead of someone else's, and we'd have two happy souls dancing on the planet. Some teammates may have volunteered to work a flexible schedule for months, if not forever. Others may have had dreams of starting a company, applying for another role in the department, or honestly sharing that they were exhausted by our intense work and needed a break.

I believe it's time to treat all workers as the adults they are, with the capacity to think, create, solve, and serve. Teams with the safety and trust to explore any topic and define their best path to the goals and desired outcomes will get there fastest and get there together. Yes, it takes discipline to plan the work before you work on the plan, and it takes time to pause for reflection and retrospection. But the relationships, dynamics, and performance that come from high trust, high engagement, and highly empowered diverse teams hold the magic that most only dream of.

ACTIONS FOR RADICALLY TRANSPARENT TEAMWORK:

1. Expand and extend forums to wider audiences. If COVID gave us any gifts, one of them was a global comfort with video conference technologies. It is very easy to open the doors and windows to many formerly closed management processes by inviting constituents to listen in, even when they do not actively participate.

   When Niaga was purchased by Covestro AG, we were asked to

present the business plan to our new boss, Karsten Danielmeier. I explained how Niaga held radical transparency as a value and how all teammates were invited to participate in reviews and discussions. I asked if he would allow the team to listen in as four to five of us presented the business case and next milestones to Karsten. I was happy when he was willing to try it and thrilled when he did not hesitate to ask difficult questions, knowing twenty extra pairs of ears were listening to his challenges and concerns. We are all adults in these roles, so I encourage teams to lean into transparency and welcome the conversations that follow presentations and debates. Most people do better work when the context they are working in is clear. I also believe policy shifts and changes that are unpopular at implementation can be shaped and debated up front if the forums are allowed. We really don't know how people feel about ideas or opportunities until we ask!

2. Take advantage of technology to enable collaboration, share work, and store progress. From Microsoft Sharepoint and Teams Channels to Google Drive, it is inexpensive and easy to offer internal and external communities space to work on documents, utilize existing content to shape new presentations, store tools, and organize policies and procedures. It is important to protect intellectual property and organize firewalls for some projects, so take governance and compliance seriously while allowing as much transparency as possible. I've watched organizations tightly control financial information, pricing and margin data, and customer lists as if every employee was likely to download the information, quit tomorrow, and sell it to the competition. A few trusted, busy people made all the decisions behind closed doors while very talented people waited for

updates and customers waited for quotes. I preferred teaching sales professionals to run their territories like CEOs, shaping territory strategy, compensating them on margins, and reviewing results in a consistent cadence.

13

CELEBRATE LIFETIME LEARNING

"There are no failures in life except a failure to learn."

—MANEET CHAUHAN

When I was twenty-eight years old, my boss was a tall, skinny guy named Mike Johansen. Like me, Mike had started his career in finance. He had been promoted to a coveted general manager role that I aspired to in my future. I had been with Avery Dennison's Office Products North America team for a few years, and I'd left my jobs in group finance and writing instruments to take a broader role in the Organization, Filing, and Presentation business team, which Mike led at the time.

I enjoyed working closely with the sales teams and category managers across the retail, wholesale, catalog, and mass market channels, leveraging my beloved spreadsheets to analyze the performance of product placements, back-to-school store displays, newspaper advertisements, and campaigns. We had decent budgets to promote Avery brand binders, dividers, sheet protectors, and the Hi-Liters, MarksALot, GlueStic, and Avery Gel Pens. Most promotional activities were cyclical, so approvals for advertisements and displays were generally routine and low-risk.

Out of the blue, the sales leader for OfficeMax called one day to share a big campaign they were creating to take market share from Staples, Walmart and other retail stores during the year's back-to-school season. An executive at OfficeMax was planning a big television advertising campaign that would be backed by newspaper circulars with hot deals and in-store displays for the related items. All that was needed was a few million dollars from the suppliers in the category and we'd be on our way. Surely, we wouldn't want to miss this opportunity!

In case you are not a binder, marker, or highlighter connoisseur, Avery was the leading brand in binders and dividers while the Sharpie brand led in the permanent marker space and Crayola won with kids' crayons and markers. Expo led in dry erase and whiteboard. Highlighters have many formats and brands. Thanks to Avery Labels, many Avery brands and categories were stocked and sold at every major outlet, but we were not always the biggest fish in the pond.

The opportunity was exciting, and our team studied the investment and return scenarios from as many angles as we could envision. We prepared a report and recommendation, and time was scheduled to review the work and ask the big boss, Mike, for his decision. I set him all up for an acceptable answer, as the opportunity was marginal at best.

As I stepped into the door frame, Mike simply looked at me and said, "You can make this decision." "But Mike, we're talking about $1 million...(gulp)." My palms got sweaty, and I felt an urge to throw up. He affirmed, "I know you've studied it, and you'll do the right thing."

I was only paralyzed momentarily, which dissipated into a quiet panic. I met our team back in our corner of the floor, and we reviewed everything again before deciding **not** to pay for the program. Our in-store displays and regular Sunday Circular advertisements had already been secured, and the extra sales lift needed to pay for television advertising and expensive promotions was highly unlikely. This was not going to make OfficeMax executives or our OfficeMax sales team happy, but the benefit just didn't match the effort or expense.

The outcome of this decision is not the focus of the story; it was the impact of the vote of confidence and the opportunity to stand for my team and our work, to feel empowered and live with the consequences of a risky decision, that has stuck with me for life. How often do we truly empower strong performers to make big decisions and let them learn through the outcome for better or worse? Can we assess which decisions truly put the business at the highest risk and allow more learning to happen with a bias for action and experiential learning by smart and capable adults trusted to do the right thing, to understand strategy, and to fulfill our mission and purpose?

In Avery Dennison's reflective business, we chose the top value-creation programs together each year. Some served the short-term results, and others set the stage for the products and tools required to win long-term. We exited categories and doubled down on geographies. We estimated impacts, assessed risks, and took our power and position back by owning the #2 market share instead of being embarrassed by our small size. We had to see ourselves differently before anyone else saw our potential and possibility, and once the momentum shifted, it changed for good.

In just six years, we launched new products, added capacity, delivered 12% CAGR and 26% ROTC. We created a category in digitally printing traffic signs, a platform that fuels growth, and shares gain to this day. We spent time with the change agents in the industry and regained the trust and wallet share of those 'problem customers' we were supposed to part ways with. We became friends with each other, our customers and suppliers along the way.

In the reflective team, everyone held the privilege and the responsibility to participate in our prioritization exercises and the execution of our work. The process involved welcoming each colleague to the table with their top ten ideas for value creation in the one-year and five-year windows. These ideas could be new product launches, geographic expansions, cost reductions, productivity initiatives, share gains from worthy adversaries—really anything. We would submit all the ideas and then meet for a workshop.

In the workshop, each person presented their ideas. When ideas were similar or overlapping, we built on the base idea to improve or expand it. After everyone had made their case(s), we went through an exercise to show support for the best ideas, creating rankings based on the size of the prize, effort required, and time to results. We were looking for no more than ten ideas to quantify and organize project plans around.

When the top five to ten concepts were clarified, an owner was enrolled, and a one-page project plan was created. Key milestones and delivery dates were shaped, and this Plan on a Page became the monthly reporting mechanism. All teammates were invited to review the top ten value creation projects each month, and these Plan on a Page were always updated with red/yellow/green color-coding to quickly assess progress, achievements, risks, and the next steps. When people fell behind, we all shared responsibility for pivot and persevering actions, as we all chose these priorities as one team.

The Niaga team also used Plan on a Page for planning work and working plans, with a few bells and whistles added. Most Niaga teams enjoyed the support of a coach. These coaches had diverse backgrounds but played an important role in facilitating dialogue, navigating pressures and pinches, and supporting dialogue and course corrections. We also shared a commitment to "TA-DA" moments: Naturally, people are uncomfortable when they feel like they are failing, when a trial disappoints, or when expectations may not be met. In a disruptive innovation venture, many hypotheses are not as expected, and things go wrong as often as they go right sometimes. With an open dialogue about risks and speed, we learned a technique to get loud and big when the going gets tough, literally calling out "TA-DA." With this safety and promise not to hide challenges and f&*#-ups, no one was ever alone on a bad day. In fact, setbacks became shared challenges, and adapting to reality or driving new directions became faster and faster over time.

LOVING LEADERSHIP ACTIONS TO CELEBRATE LEARNING:

1. Talk about the maximum amount of risk we can tolerate in the specific business we are in. If we are managing construction work zones or running reactors, it's not only appropriate but critical that there is only one way to do things with precision and perfection. In positions where thought leadership, innovation, problem solving, or assessment are part of value creation, the curiosity and creation potential of the whole organization are activated. Encourage thinking outside of the box and testing concepts with small experiments. When things go well, celebrate, and when things don't go well, celebrate learning. Enjoy the acceleration as confidence builds and higher hurdles get easier and easier to clear.
2. When it's time to pivot on an initiative or stop a program, recognize and celebrate the team who tried. Share the things they learned the hard way so the insights and experiences can be leveraged in similar projects or programs down the road. Promote people who excel in

learning quickly, driving transparency, and doing the right thing in the end. There's nothing that kills innovation and psychological safety faster than walking people out the door who took the chance to drive something new to an efficient and effective dead end.

14

FIVE-FACTOR WINS

"Scarce minds split peas, abundant hearts share feasts."

—UNKNOWN

Have you ever observed the top-down goal-setting process that exists in many organizations? The remarkably consistent brilliant advice to do more with less, deliver x% cost reduction with all suppliers, drive growth with lower investment, and implement IT upgrades at twice the speed with half the budget?

As a general manager, managing director, VP of sales, and chief commercial officer, I've been on both sides of these negotiations. These are tests of will, negotiating savvy value propositions, competitive positioning, and ultimately, testing the gap between the Pain of the Same versus the Pain of Change. In an important negotiation, both sides are grounded in data and their version of 'the facts.' Teams from each party bounce between the alignment meetings with your team and the conference rooms where you suffer setbacks or live to breathe another day. It's amazing to observe how pervasive win-lose negotiations have become as executives feel the pressure to meet internal targets and deliver the total shareholder returns that boomerang into the best bonus years.

I am a big believer in abundance and rewarding excellent leaders and organizations for producing excellent results; I'd just like to ask us to pause and look around at who we are doing all this work for in the end. Who benefits when we sit as adversaries shaping games where one can only win at another's expense?

Returning to *The Pursuit* by Arthur Brooks, I am first in line to agree that capitalism is the single greatest force to activate the community and lift people out of poverty. Neighborhoods that barter and trade their creations, feed each other from their gardens and provide care for their children enjoy self-reliance and healthy interdependence. After basic needs are met, education and commerce elevate simple clusters of residents into bustling villages and vibrant cities over time. Let's activate EVERYONE in our world to create, to serve, to share, to receive the benefits and joys of a life balancing contribution, creation, celebration, leisure, and fun. Let's consume the world's resources—which hold plenty for everyone—in a way that ensures enough left for the next one thousand years' residents. Let's feed everyone, clothe everyone, shelter everyone, and enjoy our precious time on Our Earth.

In my lifetime, plus ten years, all the plastic that has ever been created has entered the world, with >90% of it ending up in landfills, incinerators, or our oceans and waterways. Less than 5% of the bulky household and office items created are ever recycled or reused. I am a 135ish-pound woman who will personally contribute 180,000 pounds of trash to the world living a typical American life—and even more if I live past eighty.

Don't get me started on the food supply or modern farming practices. I'm a child from the Heart of the Heartland, and farming is the basis of Iowa's economy. The small family farms I lived near, where most farmers raised livestock and grew corn or soybeans, have evaporated into major commercial operations. I'm very proud of family and friends who face the risks, weather uncertainty, and volatile markets to feed the world while also being quite concerned about the quality of life for animals in confinement, the health impact of processed foods from corn and soy derivatives, and tax dollars used for subsidies when market forces aren't delivering healthy returns for everyone in the value chain.

There are places where capitalism has run amok, and many shifts have contributed to the mess we're in now. One example has been the late 20th century shifts to tie executive compensation to economic value added and total shareholder return metrics. As top executives became bound to and aligned with the shareholder base, actions to drive quarterly and annual growth in sales and profits came with bolder, community-changing actions to reduce costs and improve returns. Corporations made greater profits, and share prices grew, pleasing investors. But each wave of factory consolidations, outsourcing, and restructuring took a toll on the communities and households left behind, often with very little notice for the households with little savings to fall back on.

As quality of life changes in homes and neighborhoods, stress, fear, and anxiety rise. Real food is replaced by convenient, on-the-go options in bags, bottles, and cans. Dis-ease rises, healthcare costs increase, and expenses are passed on to workers. The security waiting at the end of a career in the form of pensions and government social security has been replaced by 401(k) accounts self-managed by unsophisticated individuals and professional managers collecting management and transaction fees, whether the returns are positive or not.

We've created a new category of workers in the gig economy. We access our neighbors' time, skills, and assets without benefits, consistency, or community. Yes, these jobs often provide security and foster entrepreneurship. They are also a second or third job for parents struggling to pay the bills and underemployed youth who have less access to job training programs and solid career prospects.

I'd like to nudge a thoughtful conversation on conscious capitalism. A return to a world where great companies are full of happy, high-performance employees who live to serve the customers they're grateful for each day. Leaders enjoy the privilege of organizing teams to accomplish great things and celebrating success while learning through failures. When happy customers pay fair prices for goods and services, companies pay their teams and expenses, and the remaining profits overflow to happy investors.

When the employees from the happy companies go home after work, they return to a home they can afford in a car they can afford or take public transportation when it is timely, clean, and efficient. They feel the satisfaction of their workday and come home with the energy to prepare and enjoy dinner, learning about their partner's day and what happened at school.

How can we move from our current state, our normal today, to a future state where we have full participation in work, play, production, and pleasure? Healthy workers with healthy families, financial stability, good health, and thriving communities in a flourishing world would be the ultimate goal. Starting with the end in mind and identifying the gaps would be a good place to start, too. That might feel like boiling the ocean, so I'll offer a simpler framework for conscious capitalism based on 5-factor wins.

Every strong P&L says Sales (Happy Customers)	-	Cost of goods sold (materials, production costs or service cost (Happy Employees)	=	Gross margin
Gross margin	-	Operating expenses (Happy Employees) and the places and support they need)	=	Net income (Happy Investors if the Happy Employees served the Happy Customers well)

There are the first three wins. How many other wins can we deliver when our mission and purpose are to use our businesses to serve better communities and a better world?

Five-Factor Wins deliver on the best outcomes we can possibly achieve for our customers, our teams (our enterprise), our investors, our communities, and the world. The agenda is not only about money; it's also intentional about the well-being, balance, and long-term sustainability of the organization, the resources in play, and the impact to the planet for many future generations, not just ours.

LOVING LEADERSHIP ACTIONS FOR 5-FACTOR WINS:

1. How broad were the wins felt when last year's results were achieved? Were the same people employed on January 1 and December 31? What drove changes in the team landscape? How many people benefitted from the achievements of the enterprise? How can you see

the waves of impact on the customers' businesses, outcomes, and employees' lives? Were there changes in the communities where operations and teammates are located? Changes in the environment and downstream users of the things we created and sold? Did we leave the world better than we found it in the year of work together?

2. Consider adapting the three-year and long-range planning activities to ask broader questions. Flag actions and activities that affect communities today and generations to come. Question their value today and encourage dialogue to shift the enterprise's activities and portfolios over time if the honest impact is not sustainable for generations to come.

15

LOVING FEEDBACK

"Feedback is the Breakfast of Champions.!?"

—KEN BLANCHARD

Like most people who have survived several decades, I've experienced feedback in many forms and from many people. The feedback itself is just as diverse as the people giving it to me, and its impact has ranged from extremely valuable—even life-changing—to utterly absurd.

At twenty-eightish years of life, I was proudly leading a small team at work. I enjoyed the work we were doing, the people I worked for, and the colleagues I worked with. We bonded as underdogs, working on the lower-margin and more competitive products in the company's portfolio. Every major decision was analyzed and modeled, and our crew was particularly creative in capturing customer opportunities.

As a young leader, I treated my teammates like family. On their birthdays, I would bake a full pan of cinnamon rolls and set up a small buffet of coffee, juice, fruit, and homemade treats to recognize the moment and celebrate the men and women I appreciated and enjoyed so much. Beyond a shadow of a doubt, there was a little internal competition between the most profitable business unit and ours. Working on the same floor of a four-story building, we all knew each other and performed similar roles, but we generally stayed in our camps for the daily grind while being cordial and tolerant in shared spaces.

I was six years into my career, six years into being peers with people generally ten-plus years older than me and actively managing people five to thirty-five years older than me. In fact, on my first day in a new role, I presented a thirty-year service award to a new direct report. I felt foolish, as he had been working for this company longer than I had been alive. How will I ever be helpful to him, let alone earn his respect? It didn't take long, though, before we were enjoying each other: My strengths supported dialogue, analysis, and teamwork, while others' strengths and experience drove insightful options, great perspectives on risk, and the speed that comes with repetition and proven track records.

The company had an annual talent review process where all employees were assessed and rated on performance and potential. I was pleasantly surprised to hear that Paul, a retiring general manager, who was well-known for his coaching and development focus, had agreed to mentor me in the year ahead. How lucky for me to have access to someone finishing a career in a position I only dreamed about for my own future.

The day finally arrived for my first interaction with Paul. I woke up early and dressed in my favorite clothes and shoes. I felt the anticipation of a door opening to the next level in my career. How cool that I had been chosen to receive coaching and guidance from one of the most popular leaders in the building! Surely, only good things were in store.

In our first and only meeting, I received a lot of feedback and guidance, which I will never forget.

First, I was told I was perceived as cold and unapproachable. Peers and subordinates found me intimidating and forceful—too serious about my work and rigid.

Please note: I had never spent any quality time with this man before, and he didn't take a single minute to get to know me, ask me any questions, or explore my experience or ambitions.

He simply shared this feedback and dispensed his two-fold action plan: 1) You should consider baking. If you were to bake treats at home, people would experience you as warmer and kinder. 2) Be more casual: Dress more casually, wear more comfortable shoes, and lean or sit on the furniture in meetings. Even take your shoes off and walk around the office in your socks or stockings. Mind you, this person did walk around the office in his socks, allegedly including the men's restroom.

Isn't it funny that one person can dispense advice like 'Dress for the job you want, not for the one you have' while another person says, 'Dress to make others comfortable with you.' And when these people have perceived power over you, who are you dressing for in the end when you make choices to change?

Fortunately, I can easily give credit to other mentors and coaches who have given excellent feedback.

A very memorable human resources leader named Vicki was by my side when I was passed over for a promotion. I was frustrated, disappointed, upset, and perhaps a little embarrassed. No one likes to hear that they're not ready or someone else is a better fit for the role.

In this case, Vicki took the time to acknowledge my strengths and offer perspective. She used the analogy of soup versus stew: After eighteen months in my current assignment, I was a very good soup—nothing was bad or wrong, but I just hadn't lived through our business cycle multiple times.

She had the wisdom at forty-something that I didn't understand as a twenty-something: Living through seasons, situations, and cycles helps you navigate and anticipate what can and will go right and wrong in the next round. She saw my potential, soothed my soul, and encouraged me to steep in the Crock-Pot of life for another year or two, with the promise that experience will turn me into the stew that is much richer, satisfying, and nurturing over time.

If a man telling a woman to bake (especially without knowing I baked regularly from my own loving and generous heart, and of my free will) is on the questionable end of appropriate or useful feedback, and an experienced professional coaching a young leader about patience, experience, and grounding is on the helpful and impactful end, feedback that is never shared falls somewhere in the middle.

After reaching the director level at my company, I was sent to media training. This training program prepares people to speak for the company and carry themselves in a manner consistent with the company's image and brand. Over a few days, I learned tools and techniques to make sure my words and expressions matched the situation at hand, as well as boundaries and best practices for communicating through print, public speaking, and videos. We were given topics to speak about and then videotaped. A valuable critique on appearance, cadence, emotions, facial expressions, and content was provided before each 'do-over,' giving space to improve and see yourself changing in each round.

During this training, I learned that I had a 'perma-smile.' At one point, while on video, the trainer prompted me to talk about the most serious topic I could recall for one minute. I launched into a dialogue about female genital mutilation in Sudan, Egypt, and other countries. In the video, I'm talking about such a serious topic with this shit-eating grin on my face. Unlike Barbara Walters or Dan Rather, my smiling face and nervous voice projected an upbeat, happy, high energy while my words were alarmed and concerned. I had no idea there was a smile on my face, as it was an unconscious, nervous response I had no awareness of, let alone control over. I was very grateful for this experience, as I never knew the intent in my heart didn't match my impact when my gestures and expressions projected a completely different vibe. What a gift to learn of this gap and have the chance to work on it with an expert!

Returning to the office, I shared the insight with my coach. "I have a perma-smile, which is a nervous response that makes my messages and energy confusing to others when it's time to talk about something serious and important." And she said, "No one has ever told you that? Everyone knows that about you."

How often do we have an insight or story about someone who could help us a lot, but we don't take the time or energy to connect and share the information? How many supervisors or leaders have you worked for that never give feedback, even when you know they sit in days of meetings every year discussing performance and succession planning?

Feedback flows in loving cultures, as it takes care and compassion to give feedback that lands squarely, connecting intent and impact with any colleague's best interest at heart. It is an act of love to see and recognize someone's strengths and an act of love to explore gaps and opportunities to improve, build skills, address issues, and try new approaches.

BEST PRACTICES FOR LOVING FEEDBACK:

1. Check yourself first to ensure the motivation for feedback is to help and support the person in mind, and not to make us feel better or relieve our own discomfort when people have a different

style, behave differently, or communicate differently than us. Creating safe spaces where diverse, high-impact talent can be themselves requires tolerance, trust, and psychological safety. Nothing kills creativity and motivation faster than judgment and criticism, so take a moment to prepare well for a dialogue that always has both the person and the team in mind.

2. Praise in public, coach in private. I believe there's no such thing as celebrating great performance too often, but there is a time and a place for evaluation and course correction. I deeply respect colleagues who carefully observe actions, behaviors and reactions before sharing feedback. These leaders honor and prioritize each teammate's development and growth by reserving criticism or crucial confrontations for one-on-one time. Processing an incident or experience in a group can be effective when the goal is to learn from shared experiences in a team setting, so selective moments for public feedback can be good for everyone. Generally, though, feedback should be an insightful dialogue and not a one-way judgmental critique. Allow ample time for feedback to be delivered, received, and explored if you truly care about growth and development.

3. Give feedback as close to the observable moment as possible. Base feedback on direct observation instead of stories or memories. Ask for permission to give feedback about an experience and start by learning from the person's experience at the time. What happened from their point of view? How did it make them feel? How did they perform in their own eyes? How did they experience the reactions of others? Is there anything they would do differently? I've frequently been pleasantly surprised by the self-awareness people already have of their behaviors and how open they are to reflec-

tions and suggestions when you've shown them the care to understand before being understood.

4. Be clear and concise about the core message and clarify what the payoff could be from a different approach or alternative action/reaction. The best feedback might sting a little, but when it comes from someone you respect and admire and who you trust to have your best interest in their heart, it will create space for reflection, consideration, and course correction.

5. Catch people doing something right. Feedback that reinforces strengths or recognizes positive change goes twice as far as feedback that is critical—"calling people out"—or punitive.

6. Pause for retrospection: Create consistent reflective conversations with individual colleagues and teams. It may feel like soft time, slow time, or wasted time to use an hour every two weeks to discuss HOW the key projects are running, how people are feeling in their own work, and to check in on the teamwork and interpersonal/interdisciplinary dynamics. In agile work, pace and productivity improve as alignment holds and psychological safety grows.

7. If you lead people, do not ask them to write their own performance reviews! Self-assessment can be valuable in organizing yourself for a good performance dialogue, but great teammates are close enough to the work to provide accurate and insightful perspectives on performance versus targets, *how* the work is being done, and the teammate's greatest strengths and opportunities for improvement.

8. Last but not least: Please stop telling women not to cry. Tears are information and a call for compassion, not criticism. Tears at work are a sign of frustration, being overwhelmed, exhaustion, or another

unpleasant feeling too strong to stay inside. Take a walk with her. Hand her a tissue. Let her breathe, and then create space for her to share when SHE is ready. Most of us are terribly embarrassed all on our own with these moments that hijack and overwhelm our emotional control. The most supportive thing you can do is care enough to see her, support her, and let her feel your hand on her back. Maybe someday we'll even be ready to hug. (Ya gotta have a dream to have a dream come true, after all!)

BONUS: MY FAVORITE 360-DEGREE FEEDBACK TOOL

While feedback processes are generally anxiety- and fear-provoking, there are few tools more useful in work and life than gathering and sharing perspectives and ideas from people closest to you. Many coaches and companies offer excellent tools and programs for gathering and sharing feedback, and I have an entire tub of surveys and assessments about me from over thirty years. I came to love feedback so much that my lists of survey contributors would be twenty to thirty people long, while I watched peers submit five names of people they had the best relationships with, hoping only to receive positive feedback in these company-sponsored 'tests.'

I'll never forget a workshop where the facilitator handed us our feedback reports and let us take a break to read and digest. Fred and I went to the same space to sit quietly and absorb the data and verbatim comments. His report was a few pages long, and I could see the green lights and smile on his face from my chair. My report was a small book, and the extensive feedback made me laugh and cry. There were comments from people who celebrated my strengths, but also critical perspectives from people who had plenty of guidance on how I could be more effective with them and more impactful in my work and life. It was stimulating, energizing, upsetting, and surprising. It was also mine to act upon—or not—as I wished.

Fast-forward over years of soliciting and acting upon rich feedback. I've watched myself and colleagues who were open to criticism and ideas grow and grow, continuously adapting and improving as professionals and humans, while those who avoided and feared confrontation or criticism stayed true to their normal, only to stagnate and take one approach from one role to another.

The 360-Degree Feedback tool I've been using with my teams for years now is distributed through Survey Monkey by me, soliciting feedback from every teammate and coach. It is only five questions, curated from the best of the questions I've ever seen on my own feedback reports. I receive and format the feedback, and I connect with each survey participant for a reflection session to ensure the strengths are acknowledged and leveraged, as most humans focus solely on the criticism and weaknesses when receiving insight from others.

THE SURVEY QUESTIONS ARE:

1. What are [name]'s greatest strengths, and what do you admire most about him/her?
2. When strengths are overused, they can become weaknesses. Does [name] have any overuse behaviors or tendencies that affect their impact and effectiveness?

3. Many people have blind spots or low awareness of actions and behaviors that affect others around them. Does [name] have any blind spots, and how could they adapt to overcome this challenge?
4. Please rate [name]'s effectiveness as a [role or title they hold] on a scale of 1-10, where 1 is low and 10 is high. Please explain what it would take to achieve a higher rating.
5. What words of encouragement do you have for [name]?

LAST THOUGHTS FOR LOVING FEEDBACK:

At the end of the day, we are each the CEO of our own lives, the solo residents of our bodies, and the beneficiaries of our own spirits and minds. We are each navigating humanity and a crazy world to the best of our abilities and predictably acting in our best interest, seeking the path of least resistance. When you're giving feedback, please do it with care, kindness, and compassion while being as specific and direct as possible. When you're receiving feedback, simply express gratitude for the person showing enough courage and care to offer it—no matter what you hear. Then, take that gift, sit with it, and decide whether it belongs in your life or in the trash. You are responsible for your actions, reactions, development, and growth, and only you can decide what is best for you in the end.

16

CHASING DREAMS

"Ya gotta have a dream to have a dream come true."

—OSCAR HAMMERSTEIN II

In late September 2021, the Niaga team gathered for one of three team workshops we held each year. We were particularly happy to be together in person, as Dutch protocols and guidelines for social distancing and gatherings had eased for a moment. The last workshops had been online via Microsoft Teams, which was better than nothing but certainly not ideal.

As I sat through the presentations, I felt uncomfortable and congested in my right arm, from my shoulder through my elbow and down to my wrist. I was massaging and rubbing it, aware that something was a bit off but not quite painful. My teammates noticed my discomfort and checked in, and I assumed I probably slept funny or something.

A week later, there was a strange lump in my neck near my left clavicle. With two strange sensations in my body and cancer survivorship in my life experience, I decided to visit the doctor during my next trip to the U.S. I'd had a clean mammogram in December, so I wasn't too concerned. Still, better safe than sorry.

Fast-forward two weeks, and one mammogram turned into two mammograms, ultrasounds, and (four) ultrasound-guided biopsies. Confirmed tumors in my right and left lymph nodes and my neck led to MRIs, CT scans, nuclear bone scans, and CT-guided biopsies. At the end of the day, a mutated version of my prior cancer had returned, and tumors and bone metastasis riddled my skull, spine, breastbone, ribs, breasts, lung, and pelvis. When the testing was complete, I sat with my oncologist to understand the situation and path forward.

With the pervasive spread of the metastasis throughout my body, the cancer was classified as Stage IV. I expected an aggressive treatment plan that would leave me bald, with a best case of better boobs in the long run and a worst case of an early demise after one helluva fight. I was shocked to learn the treatment plan following this grim diagnosis would not include chemotherapy, radiation, or surgery. The plan was simply to keep me alive as long as possible. A new drug called Kisqali was the big bet, which I'd take for twenty-one days on and seven days off. When cancer eventually outsmarts that one, we'll switch to something else. Other drugs were deployed to stop my body from producing estrogen and another to protect bone density.

The first time I'd had breast cancer—Stage 1—I didn't tell many people. It felt small, and I didn't want my kids to think their mom was going to die. The treatment plan was straightforward, and I simply took a day of vacation to have a lumpectomy and scheduled my radiation treatments after work. No one needed to know, and my partner and parents had their hands on my back every step of the way. Only now do I realize how much this said about my relationships and my capacity to receive love and support. It's ridiculous that I didn't lean on my siblings and friends to be held through something so terrifying for me and for them.

Eight years later, I had come to know the power of networks. The information and insights available around the globe were difficult to find and navigate on my own but easy with the help of friends.

I grabbed my iPhone and recorded my first video update on Facebook, sharing the diagnosis and outlook with the world. I'll admit it took a few tries to talk into the camera without getting choked up. The lump in my throat held the tension between hope and gratitude to be alive and a profound sadness that I might miss so many things I'd like to be present for in the future.

One video turned into quarterly updates as my sister or mom reminded me many people were with me on this roller coaster, riding the twists and turns together. I incorporated my story into professional keynotes. I asked for help everywhere I turned and promised to share what I learned.

Lo and behold, the help did come! As ideas were exchanged, I read the books, watched the video, called the clinics, blended the smoothies, pressed the juice, and meditated for hours. I said 'yes' to everything that made any sense to me, including hiring a photo healer in Tenerife, Spain to look at my picture and pray for my healing every day. I declared war on every source of dis-ease in my body and my life and made conscious choices to do whatever it took to be at ease, to restore my health, and to spend the rest of my life—no matter how long that was—doing things I love with people I love.

The best gifts come in the strangest packages, and I can now affirm facing the end of my life was one of the best things to ever happen to me. I will never know exactly where the credit should go for the restoration of my health or the quality of the life I am living now, but this journey has led me to this place and this book. This is my opportunity to use the life I have left to leave the world better than I find it. I had been waiting for guidance on how to serve others or contribute to something important, and it finally became crystal clear.

Fourteen months ago—post-diagnosis—I was with a group of women at Atlas Holdings' annual meeting. We were in a special session for our development, and the facilitator took us through an exercise to identify our greatest fear. After peeling the layers of our emotional 'onions' apart for a good thirty minutes, we wrote our greatest fear with a thick, black marker on a letter-sized paper. With the paper held in front of our chests, we were to walk out into the hallway in silence in search of women with the same fear.

My sign read, "I'm afraid my life didn't matter." To this day, I get a lump in my throat when I think about it. I knew I was going to die, and I had this horrible feeling that no one would notice, let alone care, when I did. I'd enjoyed a successful career, and there were many artifacts and photographs to validate my existence, but I lived with this horrible feeling that I hadn't done anything meaningful or important in service to all or to benefit the world.

I was surprised to find eight to ten people with very similar sentiments on their chests. As I looked into their eyes, I could only think, "WHAT THE [HECK]?... You are AMAZING! You are someone I admire, appreciate, and look up to! You're beautiful and kind and impactful, let alone successful, articulate, and impressive!" I saw every other peer in this circle as the best of the best, but when I looked at myself in the mirror, I didn't see my own excellence, power, or grace. I just saw a very lucky farm kid from the heart of the heartland, USA, who did not want to die alone.

This activity had a profound effect on me. It drove awareness of the real dis-ease in my life and my spirit: deep-seated feelings of unworthiness, self-loathing, shame, and grief festering inside and manifesting as physical harm in my body. With the help of an incredible coach (thanks, Shawna Reininger!), meditations, and retreats with Dr. Joe Dispenza, therapy involving psychedelic/plant medicines, and one oncologist who brought his love to work, I am flourishing today.

A second opinion at the Cleveland Clinic was one of my best Christmas gifts in 2021. My friend, Liz, worked for the Taussig Cancer Center, and she organized an appointment with the head of breast oncology. In Dr. Jame Abraham, I met an oncologist who listened well enough to get to the heart of my pain. After reviewing my blood tests, scans, and treatment plan, the Cleveland Clinic team concurred completely with my University Hospital's oncologist. Dr. Abraham took time to explain his approach to treatment now and down the road. But then he paused, looked me right in the eyes, and asked, "*Why are you really here*?"

I started crying unexpectedly, feeling the moment's greatest pain. I had been working on my estate plan, preparing to leave my assets to others, and I was feeling very sad and disappointed that I would never build or buy the modern home I'd always wanted to live in. It just felt irresponsible with the fucked up global supply chains, high mortgage rates, and rising costs of raw materials. And at this point, I'm supposed to be leaving my shit to my kids anyway, right?

He listened intently while I spoke through tears and then said, "*Kelly, you're still here, right?*" Yes. "*And you seem to be responding well to your treatment plan, right?*" Yes.

"*I have seen a lot of cancer and a lot of outcomes, and I can't tell you whether you will be here for two more years or twenty. But you are here, and you still have more life to live. If you're not spending the rest of your life chasing your dreams, what are you doing with it?*"

I sat up like Uma Thurman in *Pulp Fiction*, as if he had just handed me the keys to the rest of my life. Raphaelle Giordano has written a book titled *Your Second Life Begins When You Realize You Only Have One.* That certainly feels about right to me, which begs the question: How can I help people to enjoy their lives, activate their gifts, savor the generous present moment, and serve in the way that fills their spirit?

I'm chasing a dream right now, in the comfort of my dream home, sharing the stories and learnings of my life to date with you. I believe my life has unfolded in a specific way so that I have learned that we are all 100% human and 100% divine. As humans, we are trapped in our stories, which we feel through our emotions and interpret with our minds. These stories are our individual experiences within the collective, and our beliefs—our truths—largely separate us from the present moment, from deeply loving ourselves and from truly seeing and experiencing each other. Little do we know that while we are as human as humans can be in our fighting, judging, loving, hating, criticizing, condemning, protecting, prosecuting, treating, and terrorizing, we are also always 100% divine. No matter how human we get in our stories and beliefs, we are always powered by grace, the earth that provides everything we've ever had and will have, and the universe that expands no matter how hard we work to possess it and carve it up.

I love capitalism. I am in awe and wonder at everything we do to create things, exchange services, solve problems, build infrastructure, entertain, feed, clothe each other. We earn money with our brains, bodies, and contributions and exchange that currency for education, vacations, mobility, and experiences. Anyone can use their time and energy to do anything that is of value to someone else! It's likely there is a customer for every single thing you could possibly create and share if you ask around.

So why is it so hard for so many humans today? How can America be the richest country on Earth, and also have entire communities of homeless people living in tents in parking lots? Why is it so hard to address the dis-ease and the declining standard of living for so many fellow humans, let alone the children in our care? Why do we accept taking and taking the natural resources provided by the planet—which no individual should really own—without replenishing and restoring what is no longer available for future generations? When do we start caring about everyone as the ultimate act of caring for ourselves?

This is my chance to appeal to the people in power that I love, appreciate, admire, and adore. I'd like to ask you to pause with me. Look around at the fear and anxiety we've normalized. Look inside of the companies we are responsible for and make an honest assessment: Are we activating the full power and potential of every single person in our care? Do we know them and understand their strengths, experience, and interests? Are we empowering departments and teams to deliver on their commitments and responsibilities in the best way they know? When we see risks, problems, issues, or concerns, do we fix them from here, or do we ask for help and listen to the diverse approaches and creative solutions of all? Do we show our customers and clients appreciation and love, on top of striving for great quality, delivered on time and complete? Do we care enough to listen and strive for systems that lift employees, customers, communities, investors, and the world?

It's time to grab pencils and start erasing the stories that separate. Rethink the borders that keep us apart. Set down the guns that end human life. Build longer tables, not higher fences. Sit for a story to learn something new. Taste your meals. Hear the song. Enjoy the arts. Scrape away the plaque and calcium in our hearts and let love flow.

17

TREASURE TIME

"The best things in life are the people we love, the places we've been, and all the memories we've made along the way."

—UNKNOWN

In 2007, I was interviewing for my first general manager role. The hiring manager was a lovely British woman named Helen, and I was immediately struck by the combination of her strategic mind, charismatic style, and courageous heart. Along with exploring my resume, experience, and interests, Helen also asked about my family life and personal goals. One specific question: "How much of your vacation do you use each year?"

I had been with our company for eight years at the time. All employees accrued two weeks of paid vacation days per year for the first five years and three weeks of paid vacation days per year after five years. The policy also allowed employees to sell up to two weeks of their unused vacation time in January of each year, which was essentially an extra paycheck.

My honest answer to the question: While I had taken some long weekend time here and there, my husband and I had only taken (two) actual vacations in those eight years—our ten-day honeymoon trip to

Kauai, and a return one-week trip to Hawaii with our young children. To pay off student loans and save money, I sold my vacation time for that one extra paycheck year after year.

Helen shared her experience as a European citizen, where it is customary in many countries to take two or three two-week to three-week vacations each year. By the time her son, Dan, left home around eighteen years of age, their family would collect memories from forty to sixty different meaningful experiences together. Some of these holidays could be simple staycations or local itineraries, while others were destination trips to explore the world with family and friends. Her next questions changed my life as a human and a leader: "How many memories will your family share before your kids grow up and start their own lives and families?" and "What example are you setting for your teams and colleagues if you never take vacation and always work?"

When Helen hired me, taking all my vacation time was one of the conditions of the offer. From that day forward, it became a priority for me to invest in memory-making time, and to monitor my team's use of their vacation time to ensure as many people as possible never miss opportunities to enjoy life, relax, and recharge.

Surveys of American workers suggest that about half of them have paid vacation time and use it.[1] A fourth of all US workers have not traveled at all for personal trips in the past year, and a fifth have only traveled once. Many Americans who take vacation trips report working on vacation, whether participating in meetings or returning emails. This has only increased as remote work has become more common and technology enables 24/7 connectedness.

On the other hand, European workers typically enjoy 20 to 30 paid vacation days per year. Summer holiday periods are cultural norms,

[1] Source: Survey of U.S. workers conducted Feb. 6 -12. 2023. "How Americans view their jobs."

with most workers taking 14 to 21-day holiday breaks. Almost 90% of Swedish citizens have traveled to five or more countries. It took me some time to adjust to Dutch holidays while working in the Netherlands, as employees took holiday time and were completely unplugged to prioritize family time and rest several times each year. I came to see, though, that teammates in the Netherlands had the same output and impact over the course of an entire year of work... they just did the work differently. Sprints of high focus, contribution, and delivery were interspersed with two- to three-week periods of rest, rejuvenation, connection, and fun.

For the past fifteen years, I have prioritized play and memory-making for myself and my loved ones. As my kids are now young adults, I'm extremely grateful for the nudge Helen gave me so long ago. Without the pause and shift in perspective, I might have more money in the bank, but I would not have the seventy-five intentional adventures enjoyed with family and friends that have shaped our lives for the better. The best investments I've ever made are in experiences and memories, recognizing nothing is more precious than time with people we love. Our health is optimized when we feel connected in relationships, rested, and energized.

ACTIONS FOR LOVING PEOPLE TO TREASURE TIME:

1. Gather the facts on your lifetime: Look back on a quarter, six months, or a full year in your actual calendar and add it up. How many days did you spend working at home, in the office, or traveling for business? How many days did you vacation, and what did you do on those vacations? How many experiences have you enjoyed

with loved ones? What do your weekends look like? How would you rate the quality of your personal time? After you have the data, pause to reflect. How would you like the next period of your life to look? If you're happy with the balance and memory-making time in your life, celebrate yourself! If you desire anything different, shape a single action in a new direction. A baby step could be a long weekend away with family or friends. If you're ready for a deep dive into something new, perhaps an international adventure or home renovation staycation could check a dream off your list.

2. Reflect on the quality of your vacation time. When it is time to step away from work for a day, a week, or more, do you take calls and attend meetings while 'on holiday'? It is quite normal for American workers—including me—to get up an hour earlier than family to review and respond to email for peace of mind. It's common to take that one call while the family is at the pool or to step away from lunch when an urgent deadline looms. I wouldn't want anyone to crucify themselves for prioritizing work and professional livelihood, but I also don't want anyone to regret missing the very special time to focus on children who grow, parents who age, and our partners who might leave if we don't give our relationships a chance.

3. Pause to consider systems that support high-quality vacation time for you and for everyone around you. It is entirely possible to shape cultural norms that encourage vacation time, train backup talent, ensure out-of-office messages, and celebrate rest and recovery. Humans set most project deadlines, so work to incorporate expectations for breaks into program calendars. At one Niaga workshop, each employee created a PowerPoint slide about their favorite holiday trip, complete with photos and highlights.

Over dinner, each person took a turn sharing their experience. We learned a lot about each other's interests and families, and we left with a much longer bucket list!

4. Revisit vacation policies for your organization. More firms are embracing high-trust 'take time as you have time' policies over strict vacation accrual or use-it-or-lose-it programs. Sadly, though, many people do not take the time when the programs allow more freedom by design. The spirit of treasuring time and encouraging living a whole and vibrant life is much more important than the policy details! Make vacation time and vacation activity visible and show the way for teammates and colleagues by setting a good example: take time, minimize distraction, focus on family, and share stories on the other side. Let your fabulous experiences light rockets of desire for others, and in return, their adventures can inspire your own.

5. Vacation with colleagues! This may not be for everyone, but some of my favorite memories have been made with teammates and customers. I've ridden a bicycle across Iowa (RAGBRAI ride) with colleagues two times. I've added extra days onto international trips to visit the Taj Mahal and walk on the Great Wall of China. Adding a few extra flights for your partner and kids to join you on an extended business trip can be more affordable when your round-trip flight is already covered.

18

RECOGNITION AND REWARD

"The new Golden Rule: Treat others like ***they*** *would like to be treated."*

My sister was a sales rep for one of the world's premier pharmaceutical drug companies. As dream jobs go, this is a prized position where smart and social humans are trained on the effect and efficacy of new medications. When they are confident and competent, they live in company cars, driving from medical office to office, provider to provider, to discuss the drug and its usefulness in treating disease. Given every doctor's tight schedule and patient priority, visits must be important and efficient. These brief windows of time are often easier to capture when a rep shows up with snacks, lunch, or gear. The rep gets credit for the activity and market share gain as the physicians write scripts for the medicine and pharmacies fulfill the orders. Base salaries are good, and bonuses follow record-setting and rankings.

These companies also change constantly. Turnover can be high as sales objectives are specific and life on the road is not for everyone. Drugs come and go as patents expire and generic equivalents take share.

Opportunities to change teams or geographies move people around. Managers and teams shift, policies and procedures change, and compensation plans are difficult to implement in ways that enable a level playing field for the 'worthy adversary' peers. It's a friendly competition, but rankings do decide who is recognized and rewarded in the end.

I watched Anne face a double-bind. She is an excellent sales professional with a track record of success selling aluminum cans, medical scrubs, and commercial groceries. She has led teams successfully and enjoyed President's Club recognition and promotions. The move into pharmaceutical sales was a welcome challenge, offering a new learning opportunity, good compensation, and a weekday work life complementing her other roles as a wife and mother.

A few years into this career stop, Anne's territory was shaped in a way that made it impossible to deliver the paper goals tied to recognition programs. Her direct supervisor and sales director both assured her at every turn she had the largest territory and most potential for the biggest share gain because she was an excellent producer and highly regarded. Among her peer group, achieving the recognition goals required share gain (growth in new prescriptions above the territory base). Others with small territories and the same base share could meet their goals with fifteen new scripts per week, whereas Anne's much larger territory required 120 new scripts a week. In a very large, rural geography, seeing twelve providers could require 400 miles of driving daily.

Loving spreadsheets and logic, Anne knew her peer group was performing the similar work for similar compensation. Her absolute dollar growth and impact were far above her peers,' and leadership constantly noted her impact and achievements for the region. At the same time, she was in the bottom 30% of all performers nationally based on the established metrics and how the territories were defined.

A conundrum brewed, and the tension over the situation escalated. No matter how comfortable Anne was with her total compensation and lifestyle afforded by this role, and even though she was passionate about health and the medicine's capacity to improve lives, her inability to achieve recognition as a top performer negatively affected her satisfaction to the point that she considered leaving the company.

We discussed strategies to affect change from within. Anne organized the data and courageously confronted the situation with her supervisors. The first reactions were "*It is what it is*" in a "*Suck it Up, Buttercup*" kind of way, but she persisted with awareness this battle was not just for her. She had insight into other high-performing reps' frustration and consideration of a career change. In fact, fourteen people had left the company or changed roles in her territory alone during her first two years there.

Anne gave her leaders plenty of feedback and ideas for more effective goal management, but nothing changed. In the end, she updated her resume and found a better job with better compensation. She was thrilled when ideas shared during training were warmly received and broadly shared by the new company's sales leadership.

Loving leadership requires openness to insight and information from everyone in the organization. It requires awareness that conversations about compensation, satisfaction, and frustration require a remarkable amount of courage from individuals. And yet, rarely are people holding resentment, pain, or panic met where they are, with curiosity, compassion, and constructive conversation to explore the situation, the desired state, and the gap in between the two.

TAKEAWAYS:

1. A goal can be a meaningful performance objective, a dream with a deadline, or a completely demotivating target that drives discontent. The best way to know if the metrics and objectives are resonating with the people responsible for achieving them is to create dialogue within the team and among individuals.

2. Annual performance and development planning is not enough for a loving leader. Constant connection can be achieved through frequent interaction and a cadence of pauses for reflection without micromanaging. Schedule one-on-one meetings with the intent to connect consistently and hold these meetings on video if in-person is not possible.

3. Psychological safety requires holding space for people to express their **dis-ease,** and to meet that person where they are even when you don't agree with them. People's feelings are never right or wrong; they just are what they are until they shift of their own free will. Try to stay curious and explore with clarifying reflections and action questions like, "*If I've heard you correctly, you see the territory goals as unfair and impossible, which makes you feel misrepresented as an underperformer—which you are not—and at risk of leaving. If you were the king/queen for the day and could change things to make it better for you and for others, what would you do?*"

Attracting, hiring, and training talented individuals takes effort and time. It is in everyone's best interest to educate, engage, empower, and properly recognize effort, outcomes, and impact. Different people are motivated by different things, so the only way we can get things just right for each teammate is to explore their needs and welcome them to the table to shape win-win outcomes for themselves, their teams, and the entire organization.

19

EQUITY FOR EVERYONE

"Let's discuss the EQUITY in diversity, equity, and inclusion."

—ME

I'd like to explore a question and compare experiences and observations with you: Is there a difference between the way we take care of things we own and the things we rent or borrow? Do we bring the same care and attention to things in public spaces as we do to the things in our personal spaces?

I don't know about you, but I've never left the popcorn on the floor after watching a movie at home. I don't find chewing gum under the counters and chairs at my house. I've never taken a rented vehicle through the car wash. As I consider the relationship between humans, our things, and each other, I wonder: What could we gain by extending participation and ownership of literally anything to much broader groups of stakeholders?

Surely, I'm not the only person who prefers brands and places where I have status, points, miles, and rewards waiting on any given day. I'll freely admit my attachment to businesses, experiences, and spaces where I feel recognized and rewarded, and—Do I dare say? Yes, wait for it—LOVED. I absolutely go out of my way to support organizations, groups, and things which it feels great to be associated with. An inherent return—something good—is tied to giving a part of me to the cause, company, or crew. My investment could be time, money, recommendations, referrals, or support. The returns can be good feelings, vibrant relationships, treasured artifacts, fabulous memories, or good old cash.

As I climbed the career ladder, I learned better titles came with ***much*** better compensation. As managers became directors, directors became vice presidents, and vice presidents became Chiefs of Something, base salaries were supplemented with annual bonuses tied to this cycle's results; long-term incentives tied to changes in the company's total value; grants of company shares and other bells and whistles, including deferred compensation plans; company cars, and business class airfare. We may bring different educations, different experiences, and different contributions to work, but we all contribute roughly the same amount of our life's time. What would the world look like if we could automatically become owners of the businesses we loved buying from or if all employees held a piece of the enterprise value they helped create and maintain each day?

While I could use this chapter's words to address gender pay gaps, excessive executive compensation, or golden parachutes, I'm less interested in dissecting the current state and more motivated to share interesting and compelling examples of refreshing approaches to equity and inclusion. There are beautiful examples of deep ownership to explore, and I'll share three stories for your consideration. Ownership of anything comes with investment, responsibility, and risk before rewards. I'd like to meet you where we all have opportunities to share the risks and rewards of everything we build together.

My first professional job was with Frontier Cooperative Herbs in Norway, Iowa. Frontier sells herbs, spices, essential oils, tinctures, salves, organic coffee, and similar things to natural foods purveyors throughout the U.S. and Canada. As a cooperative, all customers were also members. The performance of the cooperative was very transparent, and members earned their share of the profits in the firm. Those funds were distributed over time, with some cash returned annually and some held for future disbursement, creating capital for operations and growth. In addition to this inclusive and customer-centric structure, activities in the organization reinforced community and reinvested profits in impact projects. Each year, HerbFest was held on company grounds. Cooperative members gathered to learn, collaborate, and enjoy common interests surrounded by healthy food, music, and fun. Our coffee business purchased beans from a group of farmers in the remote Andes Mountain region of Peru. We hired local agronomists to teach coffee farmers to adopt organic methods, and we purchased their entire crop. After exporting it to the U.S., we roasted the coffee in our factory and shipped it out to retail and distribution customers. Each time a pound of coffee was sold, we returned $0.50 to projects in Peru to bring hydroelectric power to these coffee-growing families, giving them energy for their first lights and refrigeration.

I offer Frontier Herbs as an excellent example of a cooperative structure with 5-factor wins: Customers were the shareholders of the company and involved in its governance. Employees loved presenting healthy and beneficial products to the world. Community was stronger when we connected, learned, and played together. Capitalism was vibrant, profits were strong, and a share of the benefits were returned to the suppliers and communities to improve their lives as well. What would your business look and feel like if your customers directly benefited from their participation in and contribution to the health and long-term position of the firm?

I learned about the second example while working at Charter NEX. Selling a company can involve presenting the business to many potential investors. In this case, one suitor stood out to me with their approach to enrollment and inclusion.

On multiple occasions, this private equity firm extended equity participation (shares in the new entity) to as many people in the companies they purchased as possible. As they invested in a company hoping to maximize the return on their money, they placed a bet that the firm would have the best chance of success if every employee felt a sense of responsibility for the present and future of the firm and if they stood to earn a very nice return on their investment in time and money. In one case, efforts to turn employees into shareholders extended to truck drivers—people hauling the company's products all over the region and country. Excellent service to customers certainly depends on orders being delivered on time and complete, and at a time of driver shortages, rising fuel prices, and regulatory change, having committed drivers ready to go the extra mile meant a lot.

Each driver was offered the opportunity to invest $5,000 in the company, and everyone took the chance to participate except one. This driver just didn't have the resources to invest at the time. The company's CEO personally found a way to support the investment for this last driver, and at last, every teammate was on board.

A few years later, the bet had paid off. The company's performance was outstanding, and new investors purchased the firm. The truckers made a ten-times return on their $5,000 investment, turning it into $50,000 when the company was sold. This money can be life-changing to working-class families, and I deeply appreciated hearing this excellent example.

What would your firm look like if more stakeholders were shareholders? How many times would an owner's mindset help retention, engagement, budget management, the little things that make big differences, and better balance between today's and tomorrow's results?

The third story improves equity through sharing. One marker of 'success' is the amount and quality of things in our lives. When we all work, we earn money to pay bills, enjoy activities, and accumulate things. Sam Walton had a dream for Walmart to make it possible for every man to have things only rich people could afford. Lo and behold, with scale, anyone could have a $39 DVD player in their home. Capitalism has made it possible for people who work to be people who pay and people who play.

From an equity standpoint, people certainly have different access to food, clothing, shelter, and entertainment. The founder of a sharing app called Peerby opened my eyes to the amount of stuff we all have versus the amount of stuff we use regularly. For example, most households include a hand drill. These hand drills are generally used very little, maybe once or twice per year. On average, one hand drill would be plenty to meet the needs of thirty-two households. Peerby was created to assist people in sharing their things in return for a small rent. The Peerby team learned that items borrowed for free were less frequently returned and often broken in use. With a modest amount of value exchanged, users paid attention to time and returned items in original condition.

Fractional ownership models, short-term rentals, gig entrepreneurship, and things like municipal tool libraries set people up to share their time, talent, and things. When six families share investment in a camper van used two weeks per year, instead of six families having camper vans idle 90% of the time, 5-factor wins are achieved: More families get to have camper van experiences, risk is shared, assets are utilized, waste is reduced, and free cash is available to all for other things. When we enable sharing models and embrace sharing activities, quality of life improves, communities connect, and space is opened for alternate uses of money, materials, and time. It takes trust, communication, and love to share models in practice. How can you and your business leverage sharing to improve equity, leverage existing capabilities, and enhance community for all?

20

FRIENDS FOR LIFE

"Your presence is my present."

—UNKNOWN

Neil Pasricha created one of the world's most popular blogs, *The Awesome Project*, which became *The Book of Awesome*. Atlas Holdings invited Neil to the 2024 annual meeting to sustain support of mental health and raise awareness of the loneliness epidemic sweeping the world. In his talk, Neil framed our capacity for human connection as the lifetime space to hold five to ten relationships in our innermost circle, ~twenty-five relationships with great friends, five hundred relationships with acquaintances, and five thousand memorable connections overall.

If quality of life could be measured by the amount of love flowing through it, instead of the zeros in net worth calculations, square feet of property amassed, or awards and accolades accumulated, the world would look a lot different. I can tell you that my life looks a lot different after consciously and intentionally choosing to prioritize my relationships and clean up the messy ones—starting first with the relationship I have with my Self.

I grew up in a rural community in eastern Iowa, with zero stoplights, a softball field, four churches, and twelve people in my high school graduating class. This is a place where no one locks their doors, keys are left in cars, and people ask a neighbor for an egg or cup of sugar. When someone falls ill, friends and neighbors show up to mow the lawn or combine the fields. I was raised by a large family and active community, and everyone was welcome at Grandma's fish fries.

Whenever our family's hardware store celebrated an anniversary, two counties showed up to say hello and share a bountiful buffet of thanks. There weren't any police in our town, but if a kid was making a bad decision, the parents were going to be way worse than the cops anyway. Someone always cared enough to ensure you made it home safely, no matter what. The town's fire department ran on volunteers from the community and was funded through the annual Fireman's Pancake Breakfast and Fireman's Ball. I was very proud my dad was a fireman and an emergency medical technician (EMT), "since it took courage to serve the community and to be there when the friends and children he adored were in danger or ill.

As I left the safety and security of the homogenous bubble I called home to explore university and the wild world, it didn't take long to realize not everyone knew or enjoyed the bountiful support and abundant kindness that was normal to me. Slowly but surely, I was sucked into the competition, social circles, career ladders, and pursuit of more along with the rest of the adults around. I enjoyed making friends and connecting with colleagues through work and play, yet navigating the power dynamics, performance anxiety, interpersonal differences, peer competition, and shaky ground took a toll on me and my family. I identified with the work I loved and felt comfortable analyzing, recommending, and solving. My professional life came more naturally to me than my roles as a wife, mother, and sister.

Don't get me wrong. I adore my kids and loved their father, and my brothers and sisters are people I've always loved and enjoyed. But it's easy to own the actions that speak louder than the words. I was ALL IN on the schedule, travels, targets, and teams that required my attention and energy twenty-four hours a day. When I wasn't there in the flesh, I was still calculating, creating, and solving in my mind and even in my dreams.

I was physically present with my family and friends, and I loved nothing more than throwing a great party, tailgating with a crowd before a game or concert, traveling to a beach or mountain, or dressing to the nines for a fundraising gala with a table of ten. Saturday mornings spooning with my son while watching *Shrek* or *Spiderman* and sitting on soccer sidelines or hockey benches with the other parents was joyous. Sadly, though, I wasn't 100% present very often. Monday was coming. Game time, and I was a pro.

I'll never forget a Tuesday afternoon when I was in my office in Mentor, Ohio. My daughter, Kate, had a junior high basketball game fifteen minutes away in Painesville, which started at 4 p.m. A sales director named Tom was in town for customer meetings, and he popped his head into my office to discuss a situation. Finding me there, trying to gather my things for an early exit, he asked where I was going.

"I'm heading to my daughter's basketball game since I miss so many. Finally, one is so close, and I'd really like to be there." Tom sat down and shared, "Kelly—I've been to the Masters, the NBA Finals, and the Super Bowl, along with many other rounds of golf and wonderful adventures. Now that my kids are out of school and moving on with their lives, I would give all those things up just to go to one more of their games." I was still in the thick of having two kids who were playing sports year-round from four years of age, with several years left on pitches, fields, courts, and rinks. But it had not dawned on me that this, too, will pass. And I would miss it very much.

Conversations like this are positively life-changing. Tom paused to share his wisdom with me that day, and ten years later, I can still feel his hand on my back. My colleagues were not just co-workers cranking it out and delivering the results day by day, quarter by quarter. They cared about my well-being, and I cared about theirs. We didn't always agree and didn't always like or appreciate each other in a moment, but the undercurrent of connection, concern, and goodness was always there in the teams I've served and been served by.

What happens over time when you let your love flow into every single facet of your life, and every relationship becomes worthy of goodness, connected and flowing in the spirit of love? The energy you give comes back to you tenfold. I promise.

SOME LOVING LEADERS RELATIONSHIP ACTIVATION TOOLS:

1. Take some time to think about the circles of relationships in your life. If there is a cord of energy between you and each person you know, what quality does that cord have? Is it open, easy, and clear? Is it blocked, knotted, or restricted in any way? Is it one-sided, dark, or empty? Which relationships would you like to grow, revive, or repair? Take baby steps by choosing one to three relationships to clear, build, or mend. It can take courage and energy to pick up the phone and connect, but great things are waiting as connections are restored and love starts flowing again. One of the most powerful things I've ever done, at the recommendation of a

great coach, was to call or meet with ten people I loved and ask them what it is really like to be in a relationship with me. I had to beg for brutal truth and unvarnished honesty, and tears wet my shirt, but it was the greatest gift I could have ever received from another. Each person loved me enough to hand me the keys to a deeper and more connected relationship, and the love flowed like Niagara Falls after they shared reflections. I learned to receive and connect as well as give love away.

2. Take some time to assess your relationship with your Self. How about the energy and love in your physical self, your intellectual self, your emotional self, and your spirit? Are you happy with your body and grateful for its strength, resilience, and energy, or are you judging your weight, appearance, or posture? How do you feel about your mind? Your balance and energy? How strong is your faith? Are you moving through the present moment at ease, or full of judgment, worry, fear, anxiety, shame, or blame? This dis-ease will catch up with us if it hasn't already manifested in troubled relationships, chronic health conditions, poor sleep, numbing habits, or general discontent in any form. Our capacity to share and receive love starts with the love we have inside our own hearts and our relationship with life, and there is nothing better than being at ease and ready to enjoy all the people, beauty, nature, music, and food, waiting for us all day, every day.

3. Make peace with your humanness. As humans, we have powerful minds, remarkable senses, guiding instincts, rainbows of emotions, and bias for action. The library of stories we've embraced as our truths and a driving call to pursue pleasure and meet needs through the path of least resistance are part of every human journey. Our

life of learning always includes falling down, feeling pain, learning lessons, and rising again. It is the tough stuff we face and overcome that fosters acceptance of others who are also imperfect beings, just like us. I had a coach named Gina when I was still learning about empathy and energetic honesty. She described the range of emotions we get to feel as keys on a piano. To master the very best of life and vibrate with the very best tunes, we must play all the keys, including the sharps and flats. Our ability to experience darkness and dance in the shadows is as important as flying high in the light. During the ENTIRE time that we are living and learning, rising and falling, and being 100% human, we are also 100% divine. We are always from goodness and held in grace by the pure and unconditional love that is our source and the force of all living things that ever have been and ever will be.

4. Create a daily practice of Pause. Close your eyes and breathe to calm and quiet your mind. Breathe into your heart to open this channel. Listen to the air in your lungs and the ambient noise in your surroundings, calming yourself with the air conditioner's vibration or the clock's ticking. When you find the generous present moment, listen for guidance and feel the energy in your space. If it's difficult and you're feeling very normal ants in your pants, simply focus on things you are grateful for. Identify any energies you'd like to release and gather them up in a deep inhale, pushing them out and into the world to be recycled and repurposed for something better for you and for all.

5. Play all day. It feels so good to extend a little cord of love to everything, everywhere, all day long, through a smile, eye contact, a genuine hello, and a quick text or call to let someone know you're

thinking about them. I identified my personal brand in a workshop with a women's network started by Carol Seymour called the Signature Network. I am a Memory Making Machine, and I activate this superpower by asking, "How can I make this [insert moment] the best [moment] this person has ever experienced?" Whether that means turning my kids' pancakes into a fruity, whipped cream feast, printing photo stickers for a team workshop activity, researching facts for a strategic customer meeting, or carefully considering the best approach to a performance improvement plan, it gives me great joy to make everyday experiences just a little bit better, again and again. What 'special sauce' do you want to bring to your activities today? What can you do to curate a little juiciness, sparkle, and sizzle for yourself and the people in your path?

6. Last, give yourself time to connect deeply with others. My favorite thing in the world these days is having one person all to myself without a next appointment looming. There's simply nothing better than coffee or a cocktail with one other person where I can listen deeply, savor the moment, and sail in flow wherever the moment goes. I fall in love with that friend or acquaintance all over again, and I feel the pleasure inside from the wide open and expanding cord between us. Life just keeps getting better and better, one connection at a time.

The workplace can be a powerful place for connection, creation, and meaningful contribution to our lives, our teammates' lives, our customers' lives, and our suppliers' lives. When we all give our best to the portfolios we create, the orders we ship on time and complete, the services rendered, and the problems solved, we create abundance and energy that flows to investors, communities, nations, and the world. When we love the planet that supports us in every way, ourselves in every way, and each other in every way, it's easy to shape bigger wins, clean and clear messes, and activate positive change for all.

I see you, and I love you. Let's connect and work #bettertogether until no one is left behind and everyone flourishes. I'll do my part whether you join me or not, but it would be so much better if we could all find ease, activate love, nourish communities, fuel passions, and chase dreams together. No better time to try than right now!

21

WORDS OF ENCOURAGEMENT

"You're from Good, you are Good, and it's supposed to be Good."

—MARY M

As we share an intention to be leaders who embrace love, who are loving and flow with the greatest force in the universe, more goodness, abundance, connection, and ease will flow into our companies, our communities, our homes, and our world. Over time, as we love ourselves and treasure our bodies and lifetime, while caring for the lives and inclusion of others, we can all enjoy less dis-ease, more play, and the miracles and magic that unfold when alive in the generous present moment together.

With that said, we are still humans, and humans have bad days. In our humanity, we make mistakes and step on toes. We will take chances and fail. We take turns placing ourselves and others in harm's way. We will judge each other and ourselves most of all. We might be too much one day and not enough another. There will be times when our fear, anxiety, worry, shame, or blame knock us to our knees. Days will come when we sense danger and feel the impulse to fight or flee.

Just keep in mind that these are normal human conditions. This is how we learn. It's how we stimulate our quest and hunger for freedom, balance, and ease. It is only through riding on roller coasters and being tossed from side to side, spun upside down and on the verge of purge that we truly appreciate standing on solid ground, at peace and calm in the grand scheme of everything. If our emotions and feelings are represented by the eighty-eight keys on the piano, we only live the greatest of human experiences when we learn to embrace the sharps and the flats in every octave, as all frequencies serve us in some way.

I respect every human's right to practice faith in any way that serves them best, including no faith, so long as beliefs are not leveraged to hurt someone else. I've come to believe every single one of us is 100% human ***and*** 100% divine. Spiritual beings having a human experience, and not the other way around. No matter how difficult or tough the worst of the bad days can be, my breath and heartbeat are constant reminders that there's more to the human experience than our bodies and finite experiences in time. Our mere existence is proof of the unexplainable magic that is our life force. We get to be here, having this experience, powered by an energy that just is. This is our grace, our love, and it's always there, 24 x 7, supporting us to experience whatever the human condition has in store right here, right now.

We can trust this grace and tap into it whenever we so desire. All it takes is a pause: a brief moment to stop, observe the space we all share, feel the breath moving between all of us, every molecule of water, every tree and flower, every natural food, and every microorganism sharing the interconnected and dynamic universe together. This force, our divinity and grace, is there for us unconditionally and impeccably. We can flow with this awareness, ignore it, or question it, but beyond a shadow of a doubt, it will be there when you need it.

I wish you the very best of health, wealth, connection, kindness, and ease as your life and leadership unfold from here. Thank you so very much for taking the time to explore these stories and ideas. Please consider sharing your experiences, experiments, TA-DA and A-HA moments as you step into your own loving leadership and the whole new world we will create together.

I am willing to see you, and I already love you,

Kelly

ACKNOWLEDGEMENTS

I am a plumber's granddaughter, and a plumber's daughter. Great plumbers build systems and capacity using natural forces of air, water, and gravity to keep our spaces and bodies hydrated and clean. These systems also handle our dirty laundry, our leftovers, and—literally—our shit. A plumber's mission is to keep water flowing, and to return waste and messes to nature to be cleansed, repurposed, and reused for the greater good.

It takes attention and intention to keep interpersonal energy flowing like water, and to sustain healthy giving and receiving over time. It finally makes sense to me why I find so much meaning and purpose tending to the "pipes" in relationships, and why I find great joy supporting cleaning and clearing the "pipes" in struggling teams and underperforming organizations. So...

Thank you to my beloved Grandpa Leland and my father, John, for the way Winegarden Hardware served our community and supported our family for generations. My grandpa and dad kept wells pumping, toilets flushing, water heaters warming, pilot lights burning, and appliances working for farmers and neighbors in several Iowa counties—humming big band tunes or playing radios every step of the way. They extended credit and accepted payment in baked goods and eggs if that's all neighbors had to give. My grandpa loaned me money to buy my first home—as long as I could repay him before Tax Day. I'm proud of Grandpa's military service, Dad's community service, and the abundance they've shared with everyone. Grandpa's hat hangs on my bedroom door, and I miss him every day.

Thank you to my mom, Sharon, who is a talented artist and serial entrepreneur. Mom had to go back to work after my father and her divorced, and it didn't take much time before she absorbed business practices and mastered event production to start her own ventures. From The Event Connection which brought ten years' worth of Cajun Festivals to Amana, Iowa to a Wedding Mints business, a Rodeo sponsorship venture, and High Banks Pottery, she represents channeling passions and talents into profitable small businesses. She uses her companies to fund her fun, traveling across the country to compete in rodeos even today, at sixty-nine years old.

Thank you to my godmother and aunt Marsha, whose house has always been my favorite place in the whole wide world. I only dream family and friends feel equally cozy and treasured in my home. Her decisions to seek more education, and to lead educators and school systems showed me it's never too late to try something new. I have learned so much from the way Marsha lives her love out loud. I wouldn't be who I am without her positive, generous, and 'Hostess-with-the-Mostess' example to follow!

To the family and community who raised me, thank you for exposure to what success and wealth really look like: Wealth is simply having more than you need. A life well lived is measured in friendships, laughter, and people who help themselves to the things in your kitchen. Money can't buy neighbors who appear to cut your grass or harvest your crops when you're ill. I'm proud to be a DR-M Falcon, an Iowa Hawkeye, and a Conner Girl.

My very first customer in life was Violet Silverman, an elderly lady who lived across the street in Deep River, Iowa. EVERY time eight-year-old me showed up on her doorstep selling greeting cards, gift wrap, and stationery, Violet ushered me inside for a chat and an unusually large order. My compensation was $1 per item or points toward cool stuff in a prize catalog. I'll never forget the orange pup tent she helped me earn, or the Ritz Crackers with Cheez Whiz my friends and I devoured while camping out in the backyard. Thank you, Violet, for sharing your abundance with a little girl with big dreams. My apologies to the Kellers and Wallaces who had to deal with a lifetime supply of bows and ribbons when she passed away.

I am eternally grateful for every teacher, coach, mentor, and executive who has taught me about business, leadership, and love. I'd like to specifically recognize those teachers and mentors who blurred the lines between work and life. Beyond working together to create and deliver projects and priorities in the classroom, office, factory, or boardroom, these leaders welcomed me into their lives and homes to share meals, celebrations, families, and friendship. Penny Wilson, Donnette Long, Kevin O'Brien, James Cotter, Rick Stewart, Robynn Shrader, Mike Linton, Mike Johansen, Tim Clyde, Margaret Dano, Vicki Perry, Mitch Butier, Amy Ladwig, Helen Mets, Katie Anderson, Carol Seymour, Darrell Hughes, Kamran Kian, Shawna Reininger, Craig Gunckel, Ira & Joanna Genser, Andy & Jane Bursky, and Cheri Reeve. These loving leaders have residence in my heart forever plus one day for good measure.

While recognizing coaches and mentors, there is one who stands head and shoulders above the rest. Helen Mets has had more impact on me and my leadership journey than any other professional. In addition to her business savvy and relentless pursuit of sustainability AND profits, Helen drives inclusion, empowerment and transformation. All this while maintaining balance, presence and joy in her personal life. I once described her as courageous, ambitious and loving to a crowded room in the Netherlands. It has been a pleasure to watch her rise and shine, and I'm forever grateful for the opportunities to work with and for Helen over the years.

Thank you to the teams and teammates who have made every stop in my career path a home-away-from-home. Kelly Smith, Carolyn Frazier, Clint Landis and the Frontier Cooperative Herbs Team, James Johnson, Rich Suit, Steve Keller, Nancy Wilbur, Ermie Thomas, Sean Downey, Stuart Bernstein and the Avery Office Products North America Team. Mark Kleinschmit, Anita Juby, Mike Hannington, Kevin Dyer, Dhiraj Kapur, Ashish Shukla,Mario Escobar, James Williams, Kjell Svensson, Carlo Kolker and the entire Reflective Solutions Worldwide team, Rachel Herchick, Anita Sturtz, Chad Tarkany, Bill Podojil, Scott Hornsby, Jason Kelley, Scott Noerr, Jen Grambo Hupp and the entire Materials Group N.A. Team, Chris Reutelingsperger, Monique Hendrix-Smeets, Nico Janssen, Chantal Jorissen, Ward Mosmuller, Debbie Appleton, Mike Roele, Brigit Verschuren, Sascha Bloemhoff, Valerie Reid, Michel Tichelaar and the entire, incredibly special Niaga team, Rhea-Joy Ong-Yiu, Jackie Vonken, Arjan Rensma, Martijn Antoinesse, Richard Willems, Arosha Brower and all coaches supporting self-directed work and well-being, Mike Sher, Evelyn Hoffmann, Jeff Whitford, Jackie Perez, Karen Samuel, Will Duncan, Mike Rapier, Jay Baitler, Ken Winterhalter and the entire Atlas Holdings/Iconex Team & Board, Bill Schoenherr, Steve Wirrig, Evan

Weinstein, Jack Glover and the NovaVision and Incline Equity teams, Lynn Utter, Noel Leatherbury and all the powerful lady leaders in our Atlas Womens Circle, and Niklas Reyes, Kristiina Lammila, Pete Adams, Jari Koikkalainen, Maris Zukis and the Ahlstrom team. Thank you for sharing passion for safety, loving innovation, caring for customers, fostering teamwork, and consistently delivering results TOGETHER.

Thank you to the customer partners around the world who have stayed in touch long after the deal was done and results were history. May Maurizio Petronio, Gabriele Piziali, and Tracy Tenpenny rest in peace. Jeff Osborn, Dean Wimer, John Abbott, Daniel Butz, Lars Engelke, Mike Sethna, Yvar Monasch, Jan-Joost Bosman, Don Earl, Jim DeFife, Thomas Dahbura, Scott Colburt, Brett Lauterbach, Frank Fellers, Walid Elhusseiny and so many others have collaborated on win-win outcomes, tolerated the Women's Tees, and shared growing up and growing older together. Your firmness, fairness and kindness have shaped these stories in many ways, and I appreciate you and your conscious capitalism.

Thank you to Tim Fazio, Jim Sorensen, and the Lakeside Books team for lighting my path to publishers and for your introduction to the Fedd Agency. Deep gratitude and appreciation to Esther Fedorkevich, Danielle Hale, Brittney Bossow, Ash Abraham, and the entire Fedd team for hitting the accelerator to finish and publish this book. I appreciate the flexibility of your service menu and your approach that enables authors to choose from a spectrum of possibilities between traditional and self-publishing paths.

I'm also grateful to the Record ATX team in Austin for coaching me through the audiobook process. I can't believe how experience and technology come together to slice and dice sounds and words while cancelling my Darth Vader breathing. Thank you for delivering the audio format!

I owe a huge favor to the early readers of my first drafts, so thanks to Anne Audo, Sean Kennedy, Margaret Dano, Tom Holmes, Rod Gibson, Dimitri Mugianis, Mark Kleinschmit, Andy Burksy, Zoey Powers, Anthony Dean, Joanna Genser, Rhea-Joy Ong-Yiu, Helen Mets, and Shawna Reininger for your tolerant eyes, considerate criticism and invaluable input. The final selection of stories is greatly improved by your curious inspection and thoughtful nudges.

Saving the best for last, thank you to my large and crazy family for every way we connect, care, create, and celebrate. I couldn't have reached for opportunities, taken risks, and faced failure without knowing I could *always* go home. I'm particularly grateful for Jack and Kate, who are thriving as young adults in spite of divorced parents and growing up with a part-time mom. I may have been gone half the time and missed so many of your games and events, but I've loved you every minute of every day of your lives. It means the world to me that you love me back the way you do, and the way only you can. It warms my heart that you've decided careers in business aren't so bad after all! I can't wait to see how you will use your time and talent to earn, and the ways you'll use your abundance to give, play, and gather memories along the way.

Thank you to everyone who has shared this life and shaped these stories! I'm grateful for our memories, our conversations, our confrontations, and the ways we use, "I'm Sorry," "Please Forgive Me," "Thank You," and "I Love You" at just the right times. There is so much more to see and do, and I can't wait to chase dreams and a better world with you!